# POKER TOURNAMENT TIPS FROM THE PROS

## About the Author...

Shane Smith is one of the most highly regarded writers in the poker world. In addition to being the author of the best-selling classic *Omaha Hi-Lo Poker (How to Win at the Lower Limits)*, Shane has collaborated with some of the top experts and writers in poker, including Tom McEvoy, T.J. Cloutier, Roy West, John Vorhaus, Linda Johnson, Max Stern, Byron "Cowboy" Wolford, Ralph Wheeler, and the late Tex Sheahan.

Smith has acted as the editor of two gaming magazines and has been published in *Entrepreneur, New Business Opportunities, Gaming Times, Southern Gambler* and *Card Player* magazines. As a regular player on the tournament circuit, the author has won and placed in many poker tournaments.

Smith has extensively researched the poker literature to unite the thinking of tournament poker theorists, winners, authors and champions into a comprehensive book that contains the best advice available on how to win poker tournaments. Combining that research with many hours of tournament play, the author has compiled the practical winning tactics discussed in *Poker Tournament Tips from the Pros*.

Her list of titles include, *How to Win at Low-Limit Casino Poker* and *Omaha Hi-Lo Poker*.

# POKER TOURNAMENT TIPS FROM THE PROS

### HOW TO WIN LOW-LIMIT POKER TOURNAMENTS

### THE IMPROVED, UPDATED AND EXPANDED EDITION

## SHANE SMITH

# CARDOZA PUBLISHING

Cardoza Publishing is the foremost gaming and gambling publisher in the world with a library of more than 100 up-to-date and easy-to-read books and strategies. These authoritative works are written by the top experts in their fields and with more than 6,500,000 books in print, represent the best-selling and most popular gaming books anywhere.

*Fourth Edition*

Library of Congress Catalog Card No.: 2003100596
ISBN: 1-58042-103-2

Visit our web site (www.cardozapub.com)
or write us for a full list of Cardoza books, advanced, and computer strategies.

## CARDOZA PUBLISHING
### 1-800-577-WINS
P.O. Box 1500, Cooper Station, New York, NY 10276

# TABLE OF CONTENTS

# INTRODUCTION

This book will show you how to be a winner at low-stakes poker tournaments! For a buy-in of as little as $10 to $100, you can join the exciting world of poker tournaments. And following my advice, you'll learn the best strategies for advancing to the championship table and winning the top prize.

Every aspect of successful tournament play is included here, from the four stages of play - opening, middle, late and final - to the essential 21 strategies for winning tournaments. You'll receive valuable advice on tournament procedures, re-buys, aggressive play, clock-watching, inside moves, discovering tells, plus you'll learn the 26 biggest potential tournament traps you must avoid.

I've also provided you with winning advice from the greatest theorists, champions and tournament players in the game including Tom McEvoy, Mike Caro, T.J. Cloutier, Bobby Baldwin, Doyle Brunson, and many more.

Tournaments are big business for casinos and can become big bucks for you. With the proliferation of legal cardrooms across the nation, you can find plenty of tournaments. More than 120 daily tournaments are held in cardrooms in Arizona, Colorado, Connecticut, Iowa, Louisiana, Michigan, Mississippi, New Jersey, New Mexico, North Dakota, Oregon, South Dakota and Washington. And in California and Nevada alone, there are many hundreds more.

Of course, you won't always be content with playing these low-limit daily events; you'll want to move up the tournament ladder. Poker magazines regularly advertise big-big tournaments called "Major Poker Tournaments" plus "Special Event" tourneys at casinos from California to New Jersey. These tournaments usually have buy-ins of $100 and up - way up in many cases. The granddaddy of them all, the World Series of Poker in Las Vegas, is but one. Others include Jack Binion's World Poker Open in Tunica; World Poker Challenge at the Reno Hilton; World Poker Finals at Foxwoods in Connecticut; and the U. S. Poker Championships at the Trump Taj Mahal in Atlantic City.

A note about the people that I quote in this book: Two of my favorites, Tex Sheahan and Bill "Bulldog" Sykes, are gone now. They both were fine men who helped me with the original version of *Poker Tournament Tips from the Pros*. I quote them frequently because although they have passed to the big game in the sky, their sage advice is still as alive today as I wish they were. To update my sources of research, I have added advice from world champion players such as T.J. Cloutier and Tom McEvoy and other poker pros who have risen in the ranks over the past decade.

You will learn lots of good stuff from this book, and you will also enjoy reading it. Tournaments are exacting arenas in which to test your poker skills, and if you use the tournament tips in this book, I sincerely believe that you'll have the winner's edge. When you win your next event, write me an e-mail to shane@pokerbooks.com, with the details and I'll send you a "Winner's Edge" certificate to display along with your trophies - or to fold inside your wallet with all that loot you have won.

# CHAPTER 1

# THE ANATOMY OF TOURNAMENTS

Don't read this chapter if you won last year's World Series of Poker or if you are a professional who already supports yourself from tournament wins or if you are a bona fide tournament junkie. Instead, skip over to Chapter Four where you'll find a comprehensive roundup of expert advice from the poker pros about how to win small-stakes limit poker tournaments.

But if you are new to the tournament scene, or if you've experimented with tournaments but have yet to win, or if you are planning to enter a tournament during your next trip to Las Vegas, Reno or Atlantic City, this chapter is for you. In this section, you will learn:

♠ How Most Low-Stakes Tournaments Work
♠ The Things You Need To Know In Advance
♠ The Buy-In Versus the Pay-Out Factor
♠ What Makes a Tournament "Good"
♠ How Much You Can Expect To Win
♠ Why You Won't Win 90 Percent of the Time
♠ The Real Value of Tournament Competition

Throughout each section of this book, you will benefit from the advice of noted low-limit and high-limit tournament aficionados. Their comments come from the books and articles they have written and from my conversations with them. The titles of their books and articles are not listed each time that I quote them, but rather are furnished in the bibliography.

# The Structure of Tournaments

In tournaments the playing field is even. That is, everyone pays the same entry price and begins with the same number of chips regardless of knowledge or experience. Of course, a professional has an advantage over a novice: He knows tournament strategy and how to use it to get to the final table, the "money" table, where he has appeared many times. Sometimes he even meets a novice in the winner's circle and occasionally that novice wins the whole ball of wax. If you are a beginner who wants to cut yourself a slice of that money pie, here are some basics that you need to know before you take a seat at your first tournament table.

### The Buy-In

The tournament will begin at a designated time. About an hour before it starts, players begin signing up for it by giving their names to the tournament official and paying for a buy-in, which is the basic fee that the casino charges you to participate in the event. If the buy-in is $20, the house usually keeps $5 (20 to 25 percent of the entry fee) to cover its expenses, and puts the remaining $15 into the prize pool.

You will receive an entry card with your assigned table and seat number on it. When the event begins, report to your battle station where you will find a stack of chips with which to fight. Each of your opponents will have the same number of chips (most players count them to be sure they are correct).

## A Round

Many low-limit tournaments are structured with 20-minute rounds. This means that for 20 minutes, the limits will be $10-$20 (for example). At the end of the first 20-minute round, the betting limits will increase, often to double the amount of the starting round (for example, from $10-$20 to $20-$40). Every 20 minutes thereafter, the limits will rise again.

## A Rebuy

Most low-limit tournaments are rebuy events. This means that when you run out of chips, or when they fall below a designated amount, you may buy another stack. Most tournaments allow you to rebuy only during the first three rounds (the rebuy period), not throughout the entire tournament. If the tournament costs $20 to enter, the amount it will cost you to rebuy usually is $10, for which you get the same number of chips as you did for your original buy-in. For example, if the starting stack was 100 chips, your rebuy entitles you to another 100 chips. In most events, you can rebuy anytime (during the rebuy period only) that you have fewer than your starting number of chips. Therefore, if you lose the first pot you enter and are left with 70 chips, you can rebuy and add 100 chips to your stack.

If you decide not to rebuy when you run out of chips, your tournament is a done deal. You are out of action and either out the door or into a cash game where you can reach into your pocket any time you go broke, a privilege to which you are not entitled in tournaments when you go broke.

## The Add-on

At the end of the rebuy period, you usually can make one final rebuy to add on to your stack. The add-on often comes in two denominations:

**(1)** If you have more chips than your initial buy-in, you may add on the same amount of chips that you began with, usually for the same price as a rebuy.

**(2)** If you have fewer chips than your initial buy-in, you may add on double the amount of chips that you began with, usually for double the price of a rebuy. For example, if you began with 100 chips and have 170 chips at the end of the rebuy period, you are allowed to pay $10 for an add-on. But if you have only 60 chips, you are allowed to pay $20 for a double add-on of 200 chips.

After all the add-ons have been completed, the tournament usually schedules a short break in play, at which time the officials count up all the buy-ins, rebuys and add-ons to determine the size of the prize pool. You, of course, use your break time to think over your tournament strategy and decide how best to win your slice of the pie, knowing that when the tournament resumes you have only the chips left in front of you with which to wage the good battle. This is why so many tournament players say that the real tournament begins after the rebuys and add-ons are over.

When the tournament recommences, play continues round by round with the limits ever increasing. As players run out of chips, they are eliminated from action (indeed a sad state of affairs) so that the field of competitors gradually shrinks in size. The tournament ends when all combatants have fallen on the field of battle leaving but one soldier standing (actually, he is sitting happily counting his money).

# Don't Leave Home Without Knowing

Not all tournaments are created equal. Some have low entry fees with rebuys and add-ons and some don't. Some spread ten or more tables but most don't. A few have highly-trained, efficient dealers. They all have prescribed formats and rules that you need to know before you enter them. Don't enter a tournament without knowing:

♠ What is the entry fee?
♠ What is the usual payout?
♠ Is it on a percentage basis?
♠ How many rebuys can you make and when?
♠ Is there an optional add-on?
♠ How many places are paid?
♠ How long are the betting rounds?
♠ How early should I be there to sign up?
♠ Which cash games does the casino spread?

The relationship between the cost of the tournament buy-in (with rebuys and add-ons) and its expected payout is important if you enter it solely to win money. "I look for a tournament where the payout will be twenty times my expenses," said Bill "Bulldog" Sykes, who had a 20 percent win-place record in low-limit tournament play. Another player I know expects a 10 times payout on her investment while another hopes to triple his money. T.J. Cloutier, who has won more money at tournament poker than any other player in history, wrote, "You want to get a good overlay on your money. If the win end of the tournament isn't 50 times the amount of money that you have put in it, it really isn't a good tournament for you. So if you pay

$1,000 to enter a tournament, you want to be able to win $50,000." In other words, Cloutier would expect to be able to win $5,000 if he paid $100 to play.

Your monetary expectations may vary, but I think you always have to ask yourself, "Will it be worth my time and money to enter this event?" Tex Sheahan advised that you should consider entering tournaments that are "on a cost basis par with the amount you would risk in the course of a normal evening's play." In his mind, the prospect of having a shot at a possible $300 to $400 payout for your investment of around $40 is enough reason to get into the action.

Make your own decision, but do it in advance by asking yourself, "How much is it worth to me to take a shot at this win?" Even though a prominent poker writer has stated that "it is always correct to rebuy when you go broke" in a tournament, I think there are other considerations that may affect your decision regarding rebuys and add-ons. One of them is how much you can afford, or are willing, to invest. Another is your state of mind; that is, whether you fully believe that you can win the event.

But the prize money is not the only reward a tournament offers. Experience is another type of payoff, especially for those who are rising through the ranks hoping to hone their skills enough to win a World Series of Poker bracelet. And some players simply like the action, the electricity, the competition, or the trophies and prestige. "The new tourney player will discover a poker high he didn't know existed and learn what real poker is about," Sheahan said. A few are tournament junkies whom you'll see at every event in town.

Las Vegas tournaments usually fill their seats quickly, so plan to be there early. A friend of mine arrived five minutes before they let down the gates and was twentieth on the alternate list. The next time, he arrived an hour early and, because seats were assigned on a "first come, first served" basis, he received Table One, Seat Two. This became an advantage to him as the tournament progressed because as the other tables became short, contestants were transferred to Table One, so he never had to change tables. However seats are most often assigned by the luck of the draw.

Most low-limit tourneys pay on a percentage basis, often about 40 percent to first, 25 percent to second, 15 percent to third and so on. A few pay everyone at the final table while others pay only five (or even three) places. Knowing how many players will cash could affect your strategy at the last table, so find out in advance.

The modern trend is to spread the prize pool among more players with a lesser percentage than in the past being awarded the top three spots. Many players seem to like this format because it makes the payouts less top heavy. For example, the directors of the inaugural Tournament of Champions in 1999 asked players to vote on how they wanted the prize pool to be distributed. A large majority voted to spread the money to more players, meaning that the top few spots would receive less and the middle to bottom spots would receive more.

When smaller denomination chips are no longer needed at the beginning of a higher betting level, they are removed from the table in a "race-off." The dealer deals each player one card for each of his "odd" chips and the highest card(s) dealt receives larger chips equal to the value of the smaller chips. In a 1994 Letter to the Editor in *Card Player*, a reader related the sad story of a tournament player who would have invested his last two small chips on the final hand before the break had he known that they were to be raced off the table after the intermission. Unfortunately he returned to the table dead broke! Thankfully, times have changed: Today's usual procedure is that you cannot be "raced out" of the event.

When a tournament spreads ten tables, it takes around four or five hours to complete the action. If you wash out early, you'll probably want to enter a ring game. The major reason a card room offers tournaments is because they want your action in their casino. These side games can be very worthwhile, especially if several disappointed tournament dropouts are in your game. Here's your chance to recoup not only your entry fee, but some "tilt" chips that loose losers so often fling like birdseed to those who fly like eagles and swoop like hawks.

Finally two words about what makes a tournament "good": dealers and decisions. In my experience, dealer competence and the quality of the decisions that floormen make are major factors in whether I enjoy a tournament. Because we don't often win the tournaments we enter (if you have a 10 percent win rate, you're among the best), we expect to at least enjoy them. Dealer expertise also is a factor in the amount of the tip that most winners give them. In low-limit tournaments, you might expect to toke the dealers about 5 percent of your win, while in bigger tournaments the usual amount is around 2 percent.

Good tournaments are well managed, start on time, announce betting increment increases, and employ good floor personnel and dealers who control rowdy players. And *really* good tournaments are the ones that *you win*!

> *"There are no more than ten people*
> *in any tournament that I have to beat:*
> *the ten at my table right now."*
> — **Bill "Bulldog" Sykes**

# CHAPTER 2

# THE WINNING EDGE

Most seasoned tournament players will tell you that you can't win tournaments using cash game strategies. Although mostly true, this doesn't mean that tournament winners don't use *any* ring game skills — it's just that they *combine* them with tournament strategies. Tournament winners also possess a set of personal traits that give them the edge over opponents who seldom compete in tourneys.

## Winners Control Their Actions

"Poker is a game where you have control over your actions," Doyle Brunson said. "You never *have* to call; you *choose* to bet; you *choose* to raise. You are the master." Or according to a clever paraphrase of Longfellow, "Due to circumstances beyond my control, I am the master of my fate, the captain of my soul."

Tex Sheahan thought of control as the "taciturn self-discipline" exhibited by seasoned poker pros. Bobby Baldwin called it self-control or "character." He put it this way: "It is the drawing up of a set of rules to govern your personal style of play. I like to think of self-discipline as taking control of my own actions without letting outside events throw me off track without just and thoughtful cause."

If you can continuously control your actions at the poker table, you possess the first winning trait of a champion. If you combine discipline with the following characteristics of top competitors, you should be on your way to a successful career in tournament play.

## Winners Are Competitive

"Aren't all poker players competitive?" you ask. Yes, but there are different degrees or styles of competitiveness. A *passive* competitor is one who is willing to win his daily nut in a ring game, a player who avoids taking any highly speculative risks that may threaten his bankroll. Then there is the *casual* competitor such as a schoolteacher I know, a "rock" who plays poker for recreation. Working in a profession that emphasizes team effort, he finds poker one of the few arenas in which he has an opportunity to compete with other people. These types of players are not good candidates to win tournaments, but you love having them as opponents.

The fighting spirit that you need to win a tournament is several cuts above passive or casual competitiveness. You must have the *will to win* accompanied by *heart*, the courage to make an intelligent yet risky move knowing that you may win it all or lose it all depending on the mix of your judgment with luck. Not the attitude that a friend of mine expressed when he explained why he never enters tournaments: "I'm just not an all-or-nothing guy."

## Winners Are Skillful

My uncle suggested that I leave this one out because "everybody knows that you have to be good at hold'em to win a hold'em tournament," but I just had to say it anyway: you've got to be a good poker player to sustain a winning tournament record. But here's some good news for those of you who are beginners in tournament action: Bill "Bulldog" Sykes won the first tournament he ever entered, even with two former World Series of Poker Champions at the final table. Of course the bulldog already was an excellent low-limit hold'em player *and* he knew correct tournament strategies.

## Winners Play People and Poker

Knowing your opponents is important to success in poker. Tells are major tools that winning tournament players use to learn how their opponents play. Johnny Moss, who won the World Series of Poker in 1974 at age 68, played people-poker. "Eight outta ten men, I play with 'em long enough, I can tell when they're bluffing. They got a tell. You get the reaction, the conversation. You have to learn what kind of hand this guy shows down, watch that one's moves, watch the veins in his neck, watch his eyes, the way he sweats."

Most top tournament competitors have an uncanny ability to "put a make" on new players within a very short time. Against many of them, it is as though your cards have no backs. They are well versed in detecting tells, as well as myriad other character clues. T.J. Cloutier is among the best. "I once took a friend who didn't play much poker to a game with me. He noticed me talking to a guy across the table while a hand was being played. 'How can you tell what's going on if you're talking?' he asked me. 'If a wing fell off a gnat at the end of the table, I'd see it,' I told him." T.J. was trying to explain to his friend that you must be alert all the time. "You've gotta be able to sit down at a table with people that you've never played with in your life and after 15 minutes, know how each one of them plays — whether they're aggressive, whether they're passive, how they play early position, middle position, late position. You have to get an initial line on their play."

You'll be able to detect very few tells, however, against professional players, as they have eradicated most of them from their behavior. Your time is better spent observing your other opponents. Several tells that less sophisticated players unconsciously practice are outlined in Chapter Seven, "Poker Potpourri," which also includes techniques to help you put a player on a hand.

## Winners Prepare Mentally

In his audiocassette album *The Psychology of Winning,* Dennis Waitley outlines the extensive "mental rehearsal" techniques which astronauts use before they embark on a mission to the moon. Just as an actor memorizes his lines and rehearses his moves before he goes on stage, astronauts "see" themselves making all the right moves necessary to a successful journey into space. Mentally, they land on the moon before they leave the earth. Like the astronauts, many superior tournament players also stage a mental rehearsal before they make their buy-ins. Four powerful techniques that you can use to prepare psychologically for your next tournament are these:

### What did I do right?

Recalling your last tournament success, you write down the effective techniques you used to win. You *feel* the confidence you felt then. You mentally reconstruct your best moves to rekindle the fires of confidence for the new fray. Then you visualize yourself at the final table holding the trophy and the cash, a technique that octogenarian tournament winner George Elias recommends. Why not? That's where it's at, right?

## Where did I go wrong and how can I do it better next time?

Recall the painful moves you made, but instead of flogging yourself, flag a better play in your mind's eye, saying "The next time I am in X-situation, I will _____." In other words, you become your own teacher to your poker-student self. Many of the answers we are looking for in life are within our reach if we but plumb the depths of our own wisdom to find them.

## Take an expert to lunch.

For the meager price of a casino meal, you can learn more from an experienced and trustworthy tournament player than you can from ten tournaments' worth of unevaluated experiences. I know: I've "bought" a million dollars' worth of tournament advice for a few $4.95 casino lunch tickets. After your learning-luncheon, write down every morsel of advice the expert has given you to munch on for your next tournament appetizer.

## Take thirty.

Thirty minutes of down time, reading time, review time, music time — whatever gives you the mind set necessary to play your best. One of my friends reads *Omaha Hi-Lo Poker* (yes, I'm plugging my book!) before he begins to play, even though he's already read it many times, to "review his mind," as he puts it. Another prefers Stravinsky to Sklansky so he listens to classical music to quiet his poker palsy before a tournament. Visualize the strategies that you plan to use in each stage, how you will play when you're low on chips, how you will play a big stack, and of course, how you'll handle playing heads-up at the final table.

> *Try to decide how good your hand is*
> *at a given moment.*
> *Nothing else matters. Nothing!*
> — **Doyle Brunson**

> *You don't need a big hand,*
> *just the best hand!*
> — **Tom McEvoy**

## Winners Know Tournament Techniques

"Poker is one of those rare endeavors in which amateur and professional meet on identical turf," Brunson said. His wisdom is as true of tournaments as it is of the high-stakes, no-limit hold'em games that he plays regularly. Novices and professionals alike are out to win the gold in tournament competition, with no handicapping as in golf or the ponies. In other words, the playing field is even.

In my Texas hold'em tournament debut, I was fortunate enough to make it to the final table in about fourth chip position. But because I hadn't the foggiest clue about correct tournament strategy, I made two errors that cost me a payout of between $500 and $1,500. First, I entered a multiway double-raised pot in fifth position with A-K offsuit against two other big stacks and two short ones. Not a bad hand, but not a good move either. The other big stacks and I lost the pot to middle suited connectors that made a straight on the end, moving me into sixth spot and the winner of the pot into third.

Had I been aware of the tournament maxim, "Stay out of major confrontations against other big stacks in late play," I would have bowed out and allowed the other two tall stacks to take out either the short stacks or each other. Three hands later in the small blind, I called the big blind's heads-up raise with 10-7 suited, throwing in my last three "odd" chips. The player who was next in line to take the big blind had only enough chips to post the blind and the next player had but one chip in front of him. I could've passed the raise and taken the button on the very next hand, virtually assuring myself of a fourth place payout in a five-spot tournament.

Knowledge is power! The tips and techniques in this book will help you avoid these types of beginner mistakes and win your share of the roses much sooner than I did.

## Winners Can Concentrate At Length

"I was so tired, I just gave it away," Joe admitted later. "I couldn't concentrate any longer. Guess I shoulda gone to bed earlier last night. We'd been playing for about five hours and around midnight, I knew I was losing it — not the tournament, my concentration. I got lucky and hung on for fifth place, but if I'd been more alert, I think I could've taken it all."

Concentration. Is that the word? Or is it commitment? Commitment to sitting "forever" in a long session. There are times when my temperament is not geared to that degree of stick-to-it-ness, when I'm not willing to concentrate single-mindedly on any one thing. That's a good time not to be competing in a tourney. Patience. Is that the word? The patience to wait when you need to; the commitment to act when you have to; and enough concentration to know the difference between the two. That's it.

## Winners Can Handle Stress

We all have a degree of tension at which we perform best. Every personality type functions at its own unique, optimal level of stress. People under no stress are either laconic or dead. Those under mega stress become hyper. Stress may get Paul's juices flowing but turn saliva into sawdust in Peter's mouth. And the things that stress Paul may not bother Peter. Do loudmouths push your buttons? Smokers? Incompetent dealers? Whiners? Women in low-cut dresses?

If stress turns you on, tournaments could be your bailiwick. But if you tend to crumble under the combined pressures of rapidly decreasing time and constantly increasing betting limits, ring games may be more up your alley. When Socrates admonished "Know Thyself," he could've been suggesting that you should be honest with yourself about the degree of stress you desire and *need* to perform well.

Stressors in tournaments include the behavior of other players, the (in)competence of some dealers, a fear of losing, intimidation by fast players, making huge bets when the limits become b-i-g, chain smokers or whatever pulls your chain. A player I interviewed for *Card Player* magazine told me about the extreme stress that he felt when he sat down at a tournament table when he was still a novice and saw five "bracelets" (World Series of Poker winners) push in their antes.

Distractions also cause stress. Playing in a Downtown Las Vegas low-limit tournament once pushed all the buttons on my stressometer. Buying in for $15 in a ten-table Omaha high-low tourney, I was sitting to the right of a maniac who kept yelling derisive comments to his buddy at the other end of the table. Somebody threw a tournament chip toward him, along with a few remarks about "table thieves." This antic prompted a rather pious player to empty a plethora of colorful contents from her Gucci handbag right onto the green felt to prove that she wasn't the culprit with the felonious fingers!

The dealer, who had complained earlier about having to work on his night off, was unable to handle the turmoil and the tournament director did nothing to calm the natives. Meanwhile, the clock ticked off the rapidly escalating 20-minute betting rounds. Contrary to the poker-author gurus who advise that it is almost always correct to rebuy when you go broke, I broke for the door as soon as I got broke. (This casino no longer runs daily tournaments — I think I know why.)

# Winners Get Lucky

My favorite tournament quote comes from Mike Caro: "Great Tournament Truth: The winner of a tournament *always* got lucky." Maybe I like this because when I lose, it consoles me and when I win, it keeps me humble. Baldwin said that "Winning any of the events in the World Series of Poker requires a rare, harmonious combination of positive factors: control, no flagrant mistakes in judgment, more than your share of luck, and the circumstances to make the whole thing work."

Luck is important in a tournament because you need it in the *short run* rather than the long run, and the closer to the end of the tournament the better. Because it is at that final table, on that final hand, that you *must* win the chips to haul in both the bounty and the bucks — plus maybe a big bomber of a trophy.

*I won or placed in the first few seven-card stud tournaments that I ever played by simply adapting the tournament style of play that I had used in other games, a style that is completely different from side games. You see, no matter what the game is, when you hit the final table, the real game is still tournament poker.*
**— T.J. Cloutier**

*General tournament strategy can best be characterized by two words: discipline and opportunism.*
**— Michael Cappelletti**

# CHAPTER 3

# THE FOUR STAGES OF TOURNAMENTS

The stages of a tournament are somewhat like the seasons in a year. In the summertime, we are optimistic, playful, *fast*. Then enters the fall when summer's leaves begin to fade and we must *slow down*. The winter wind blows in, freezing us into a cocoon of **survival**. Finally, spring dances by with new hope and we can *move* again.

In the opening stages of low-limit rebuy tournaments, many players act like children at the beach — they play a lot of hands, loosen their opening standards, raise frequently, and do their best to build tall stacks. They play fast, pushing small edges to the limit, because they know that if they lose all their chips they can replace them with a rebuy.

And then the rebuy period ends marking the beginning of the middle phase of the tourney. Most players slow down their actions and become a parade of automatons systematically marching through the rapidly increasing betting increments. They engage in sporadic skirmishes for pots that will give them a competitive stack of chips to battle with in the tournament's later stages.

Late in the tournament, players with short stacks either enter a period of hibernation in their survival cocoons, or push the envelope in a do-or-die effort to build up their stacks for the final conquest. Most players pull their A-games out of their back pocket and begin to play very solid poker. Lady Luck visits a few fortunate competitors, but as many as seventy-percent are exiled to the rail during this stage.

Finally there are but enough seats left for a baseball team and the last nine soldiers begin sparring for position, some forcefully attacking the weak spots, others tiptoeing through the mine fields of rising increments and forced blinds. The final survivors of the tourney's twists of fate will rake in their fixed percentages of the chip pool. One of them may squirrel away enough for his entry fee into the next edition of poker's version of the four seasons.

This chapter discusses the strategies that winning players use to survive and thrive in each stage of the tournament. It will teach you:

♠ The Stages of Rebuy Tournaments
♠ Goals to Aim for in Each Stage
♠ The Importance of Timing Your Moves
♠ How to Design Your Tournament Strategy

## Opening Stage

**GOALS:**
♠ **Increase Your Stack Size**
♠ **Get a Handle on the Field**
♠ **Rebuy as Seldom as Possible**
♠ **Advance to the Next Stage**
♠ **Learn Something Valuable**

In the opening stages of most low-stakes rebuy tournaments I have entered, people are playing looser than they expect to play in the later stages. In fact, some of them are *maniacs*, taking long shot chances in hopes of building a big stack to take into the later rounds. Of course, they've also brought along enough money for multiple rebuys.

It is not unusual to sit at a table where pots are raised before the flop, followed by additional raises on each betting round. If there is a maniac at your table, expect this type of fast action until the rebuy period is over or until he runs out of rebuy money. "Although kamikazes can terrorize a table, like their namesakes they usually go down in flames," is Bobby Baldwin's read on this style of very aggressive and sometimes loose play.

During the rebuy period, maniacs live their finest hours. Most low buy-in tournaments (those with buy-ins less than $100), in fact, remain "maniac" through most of the tournament. One reason that you see so many people playing loose as a goose in small hold'em and Omaha high-low tournaments is because that type of play can win some big pots. "But Fast Eddie will give it back the same way he put it in. Some guys never back off. You don't play the aggressive guy's game with a marginal hand," advises Ron Limuti, formerly a Las Vegas dealer and now a professional poker player. Your best defense is staying out of the way of maniacs most of the time, entering the pots they are in (and they're in most of them) with only premium hands. D.R. Sherer adds another tactic: "First you get your hand — then you get your man. After you have made the hand, do not slowplay it. Bet it. Why? Because the maniac will not cleverly bluff at your check. In fact, he is more likely to raise your lead bet. Make the hand and bet it out. Direct play is the key."

Rocks like freeze-out tournaments in which they play very tight up front and usually will loosen their play only when they have a big stack of chips. Some of these rocks enter rebuy events and play the same strategy that they employ in freeze-out events (those with do not allow rebuys). Very tight play in a rebuy tournament often leads rocks to the same destination as maniacs — the rail. Maniacs get there faster and rocks get there cheaper.

Selective aggressiveness is the strategy that most tournament winners and theorists recommend for these early stages. Mike Caro: "When planning to rebuy, it's best to play aggressively early in the tournament." Playing fast or aggressively is not the same as playing loosely. For example, suppose you hold a hand such as A♣ 5♦ 8♥ J♠ in a middle position in Omaha high-low. A player raises in front of you. If you call the raise, that is playing loosely. Now suppose you hold the same hand on the button against only one caller in front of you whom you know to be a weak player, with only the blinds left to act behind you, and *you* raise — that is playing selectively aggressive. In other words, select both your spots and your opponents when you plan to play aggressively.

Not all the experts agree that you should play fast or aggressively in the early tournament stages. Tom McEvoy believes that, "In the beginning stages, players often tend to play too fast, especially in the smaller buy-in tournaments." Bill Sykes added, "The people you play against determines how you should play, not necessarily 'play fast' just because it's early in the tournament." Some people prefer playing as many hands as they can as cheaply as they can; therefore they do not raise very often before the flop.

The principal goal of playing fast in the opening stages is to build your stack high enough to be able to play more competitively in the middle stage of the tournament. You are playing some drawing hands that depend upon an element of luck to be successful, so that you can reduce your risks in the later stages when you will be playing more conservatively.

The major pitfalls of early fast play are having to make several rebuys when you aren't lucky with your draws — and crossing over the line into loose play where you push the edges with inferior cards hoping for a miracle catch.

I usually play in Omaha high-low tournaments where most of the pots are multiway, whether or not people are playing fast, tight or loose, so I'm usually getting maximum value no matter what. Playing fast sometimes requires multiple rebuys, perhaps more than I am willing to make. Therefore I suggest playing a conservative style of poker most of the time. Not tight, not loose, just *solid*. (Except that when I have an excellent wheel or other draw to the nuts and I am in premium position in an Omaha high-low event — look out!)

The goal is to double or triple your stack size by the end of the rebuy period, which is usually three betting increments away from starting time (about an hour into the tournament). In seven-card stud, you may use a similar game plan except to occasionally play aggressively with a strong front against tight players who will fold a hand. Don't try this very often against weak or inexperienced tournament players because they seldom lay down a hand.

Getting a handle on the players at the table is also very important in determining how you will proceed with a hand. In the small club tournaments where I cut my teeth, I already knew most of my opponents because I played against them frequently. In the larger Las Vegas tourneys that have 70 to 100 contestants, most of whom I don't know, I concentrate on the playing styles of the better opponents. Trying to figure out how the beginners play is often a waste of time because even *they* often don't know what they're going to do next — although I am grateful for the contributions that they so often make to my welfare. If you are one of those beginners, take the techniques in this book to your next tournament table and you can feel fairly confident about your play. Then you too can feel the same gratitude for the gifts that "they" (those uneducated novices) often donate to *your* well being.

I recall an Omaha high-low tourney in which a player called every flop and stuck in the pot until the end almost every hand. After thirty minutes, he had a high stack of chips and a big smile. Just after he won the low half of a pot with an 8-2 offsuit, another competitor asked this calling station, "Why did you stay in that pot with your hand?" He answered, "So what do I know? This is the first time I've ever played this game!" Right after the break, he busted out and headed for the $4-$8 hold'em table. Players like that are hard to read.

Reading players becomes further complicated when you have to make several table changes with a constantly changing cast of players. When you're moved to a new table, look for the player who has the most chips. He must be doing something right, so try to watch him first. The easiest thing to do is to count how many hands each opponent plays to get an idea of how tight or loose he is. Then kick in with some of the methods for reading opponents' hands listed in Chapter Seven.

Some players believe that it is important to try to knock out the short stacks during the early rounds if you have enough stack power to do it, but I don't think that is good advice. Most people enter rebuy tournaments planning to rebuy several times; therefore they will not get out of a pot simply to conserve chips. In fact, having a short stack is sometimes reason enough for them to stay in the pot. Therefore my major goal is building up my chips rather than trying to knock people out.

The early rounds of a tournament set the stage for the longer middle session. Playing fast in this relatively inexpensive period can be a profitable strategy in building a cushion of chips for later, although there also is much to be said for playing conservatively. Different strokes for different folks — there is no one way to play, just as there is no one way to dress. After acquiring the full wardrobe of tournament strategies, select what best fits your temperament and style of play.

*Skill is important in tournaments.*
*If you're three times as good as other opponents,*
*you might expect to win*
*one tournament out of a hundred.*
— **Mike Caro**

# Middle Stage

GOALS:
- ♠ Double Your Chips
- ♠ Make It To The Next Level
- ♠ Avoid Making Mistakes
- ♠ Learn Something Valuable

Enter the fall, the middle stage of the tournament in which the action usually slows and the pace can become tedious. Because the time for rebuys and add-ons has elapsed, players are more conservative, settling in for the long haul. "The real tournament begins when the rebuy period is over." So goes the conventional wisdom of seasoned rebuy tournament players. I suppose they're partly correct but they are partly wrong too. The way that you have played, the luck with which you have been blessed, and the money that you have won in the first stage are the things that have brought you this far.

At the World Series of Poker (a freeze-out event), this is the stage when railbirds leave the stands to play those exciting nickel slots and weary cameramen take their dinner breaks. Players appear to be taking a nap, or are they laying a trap? They sometimes look like so many waifs indolently waiting for a handout from Lady Luck.

Although you want to "double up or get up" with a short stack, as McEvoy expressed it, still you want to avoid any unnecessary mistakes. Therefore you play solid poker, taking only the best draws and playing fast only with nut potential. During this phase, temper your play according to the style of the other players at your table and the size of your (and their) stacks. If they are aggressive, tend to lay back and wait. If they're tight, play more assertively. "If you have a large stack, or at least more than you bought in with, keep your gambling to a minimum," advises McEvoy.

I have seen players become too loose with a big stack, as though the good fortune that helped them amass so many chips would never reverse itself. They begin wasting chips by playing marginal hands and before long, their big stacks have shrunk into little lumps. Trying to parlay marginal hands into magical mounds of chips is often a big chip-waster in tournament play.

With a short stack in the middle stages, be more aggressive. You don't have a lot of time left to build a reserve for the final stages, so you play somewhat faster with your good hands to try to win more chips. With a big stack, enter pots against short stacks who are aggressive only if you have a playable hand. If you have a medium stack, tread the thin line between conservatism and fast play, leaning toward assertiveness to try to win one or two more hands that will load your guns with enough ammunition to take a shot at the bull's-eye in the final stages.

Whether your stack is high, average or low, you're trying to position yourself in this middle stage to make a run for the roses. Use your best judgment to determine your optimal strategy, depending on the size of your stack and the playing style of your opponents.

*Losing is like smoking — it's habit forming.*
*But loss is inevitable. The question is how much you can*
*control it. A winner is first and foremost a controller.*
— **Puggy Pearson**

*There comes a time in a tournament when*
*I am inside a fish bowl. It is my world.*
*That's when you can do things right — intuitively.*
— **Bill "Bulldog" Sykes**

# Late Stage

**GOALS:**
- ♠ **Survive To the Next Level**
- ♠ **Win More Chips**
- ♠ **Eliminate Opponents**
- ♠ **Learn Something Valuable**

You have waded through the tedious middle stage, looking on confidently as many others have left the fray for happier hunting grounds. Hopefully, you now have a competitive-sized stack that will help you make a grab for the brass ring at the final table. But you usually will have to make your way through these late stages by outplaying and out-lucking around fifty-percent of the original tournament entrants. In other words, the field has been pared down from coconut size to orange size, not from coconuts to limes. Ideally, you have positioned yourself favorably so that you have enough chip power to make a run for the money in the final stages.

If the tourney began with ten tables, you will need to move through about five of them in the final rounds. Approximately two-thirds of the time that it takes to complete the tournament has already elapsed. If any of the maniacs are still alive, you often will see them slow down their play (if they are smart maniacs). People begin to play tighter now, especially in the opening hands of the final stages, thus making it a prime time to perhaps run a steal. Solid poker becomes the order of the day, mixed with changing gears, timing, surviving such obstacles as all-in calls, and reading opponents.

With a big stack, you have far more latitude in your choice of play, of course. But if you are incubating a short stack, you have to go into your survival mode, playing very carefully so that your patience can hatch one big pot. "If you're wrong before the rebuy, you're still in. If you're wrong after the rebuy, you're out. Be careful!" Bill Sykes advised me. Tex Sheahan added, "This is the time for tedious jockeying, patience and more than that — iron control. Well-timed bluffs and high-percentage betting on the come are big league moves in this phase. So is opportunistic running over the game. But they all require a high stack to accomplish it."

If you are in the late lead, you are well advised to change gears and become more conservative than you were with the aggressive play it probably took to build up your big stack. Now you want to avoid matching wits with other tall stacks and concentrate your attention on small, vulnerable ones. Throw away marginal hands and try to let your opponents eliminate each other.

This is the hour of power for solid play. As T.J. Cloutier wrote, "In the first few rounds of a tournament, people usually try to play their best games, but over a long period of time, they're going to play their regular game." You will not be one of those lazy tacticians. You are a disciplined player who constantly adjusts to changing circumstances. "You have to be very careful and know how the player is playing at any particular time in the game," Cloutier continued. "Some players come out of the shoot firing and never change their style. They play the same from start to finish." Part of your mission is to determine who is playing his A-game and who is not, who has changed gears and who is coasting.

Survival tactics are essential in this late stage. Your primary goal is to *survive* so that you can *arrive* at the final table. Nothing annoys me more than bombing out of a tournament in one of the next-to-last betting rounds before the final table. I recall one especially infuriating instance when I flopped trips with a low draw in Omaha high-low and the tournament leader hung on with pocket aces to grab the case ace on the river and race me out in twelfth position, just two spots away from getting a payday. Somehow, this wounds my ego more than going out first or second.

You will be reluctant to take big draws because of the risk of being knocked out of action if you don't make your hand. You won't be betting for full value, but will be content with accepting a smaller profit to avoid the larger risk of being eliminated. Goal: Get to the final table!

## The Final Table

GOALS:
- ♠ Win the Tournament
- ♠ Win Place Money
- ♠ Survive the Cut
- ♠ Learn Something of Value

Is skill the secret to success, or is it luck? A combination of the two? Or is it what Sheahan called "circumstance" — the blending of skill, luck and *timing*, "the key time when the big stacks are in the center of the table, when that river card has to come up for you!" Like when you get a flop that hits not only you, but also three other players — except that they cannot possibly have the nuts because only *you* hit it exactly on the nailhead.

At the final table, you must catch cards at the right time and in the right place to win the tournament, *and* know how to handle them when you get them. "No matter what the game is," T.J. Cloutier said, "when you hit the final table, the *real* game is still tournament poker."

Few low-limit players are aware that it sometimes takes only a weak hand in the right spot to win a huge pot and a big tournament. In fact, the tougher the opposition, the easier it is to win by playing correct strategy with weak hands. (This is because strong players are more apt to fold when they think they're beat than weak players.) It's the *timing* that counts. A "Doyle Brunson" is poker slang for a 10-2 offsuit, total rags in Texas hold'em. Yet with that hand at *the right time*, Brunson won the World Series of Poker in 1976. Even more astounding, he won it again in 1977. His hand? 10-2 offsuit!

Although you are hoping for the right "circumstance" to carry you over the top at the final table, rely on solid hands, especially with a big stack. With an average stack, throw away mediocre hands and wait for the correct timing, trying to avoid going up against the tall stacks. Players on a short stack usually have to survive a blind or two to come in for the money. Some of them will correctly gamble more (poker *is* a gambling game, right?) with their short stacks than they would with a big stack. "If you're one of the short stacks when it gets down to five or so players, you have to find a hand that you like and just go with it," Cloutier advises. "The main thing that you cannot do is to let yourself get so short that the next time you have to post a blind, it will eat up all of your chips."

Always be aware of your relative stack status and use it as a yardstick (or a weapon) to measure the merit of your alternative plays. Observe your opponents closely. If the short stack is conservative, target him for a steal with your high stack. If the big stacks are laying back waiting for a primo hand, play more assertively in hopes of building up your chips for a higher payoff. And become aware of those players who have taken this advice too seriously — and consequently guard their stacks as though they were solid gold thermometers dictating the heat or cold of their betting actions.

Try to always play hands that can win the pot on the flop in button games, or hands with strong fronts and live cards in seven-card stud. Avoid middle suited connectors in hold'em and hands such as 3-4-5-6 in Omaha high-low.

But don't wait forever because the blinds and antes are escalating so fast, your ship could run out of wind before you ever hoist its sails, especially in seven-card stud when you can be anted out *with or without* action on your part. I recall a tight player who had enough chips left for only one more ante in seven-card stud. Holding A-J-5 offsuit, he passed the hand because it seemed too weak to enter the pot. The next round he was anted out of play. Play your A-game and be as aggressive as you can get by with and still survive.

Remember too that you don't necessarily have to break everyone at the final table single-handedly.

When Tom McEvoy first began playing tournaments, he admits that he once got to the final table in good chip position and, "seeing that everybody was playing passively, I took it upon myself to bust people out of the tournament. I took risks against the short stacks and then I got sawed off. I may have been better off by not knocking out as many people, by being more selective and a touch less aggressive. You see, you usually get a lot of respect by playing aggressively in shorthanded play, but because I had been playing a ton of hands before the game got shorthanded, my image had changed and my opponents didn't give me as much respect as they had earlier. Now they were willing to mix it up with me, to go after me." They got him that time, but Tom learned enough good lessons from his early play to win the World Series of Poker championship event in 1983. Cloutier's advice is, "Wait and let them break each other."

Bob Ciaffone wrote these remarks in *Card Player* about the 1991 World Series of Poker: "Brad Daugherty's victory shows that there is room for more than one style of play in reaching poker's loftiest crown. Daugherty does not fit the mold of aggressiveness. He does not put down a lot of heat on the other players. His poker skills lean toward solid qualities. He plays only good hands and has a fine feel for avoiding trouble." As Cloutier put it, "There is a basic tournament formula or strategy, but then you have to adjust it for your own cubicle, for the way that you play your cards."

# CHAPTER 4

# 10 TOURNAMENT TIPS

I was born to make lists. Actually, I inherited the trait from my grandfather who wrote lists of Things To Do, Things Not To Do, even Things I Should Do. When he passed away, he probably left a list titled Things I Wish I'd Done (the most painful list of all).

The basic concepts and strategies that you need to know in order to become a successful tournament poker player are so fundamental to professional players that they take it for granted that everyone knows them. Not so. Figuring that novices would appreciate having the fundamentals of tournament play organized for them in clear English, I began compiling a list of tournament tips.

I gathered the following tournament concepts, strategies and advice from an extensive research of the books and articles written by professional poker authors, interviews with poker tournament winners, my own tournament experiences, and extensive charting of live play in low-stakes poker tournaments in both Nevada and California.

The next two chapters present the best tournament advice available — tips that can change your tournament experiences from fiascoes to fanfares (Grandpa also liked alliteration). Read 'em and reap.

# TIP 1: Design a Strategy

Before you enter a tournament, design your strategy. If you intend to rebuy, decide how many rebuys you can afford and the conditions under which you will make them. For example, "I will rebuy early if I don't have enough chips left to play the next hand to the river; I'll add on only if I need to; I will rebuy if weak players have the tall stacks," and so on. Also plan your table-play strategies in advance — assertive early, survival late, attack short stacks, lay back with a low stack, and so on. Then stick with your plan for as long as it is working for you.

After formulating a strategy, try writing it on the back of a business card and taking it to the table with you. When you take a bad beat or find yourself getting crazy, refer to it to keep yourself on track and off tilt. Your strategy card also will come in handy as fatigue sets in because it will remind you not to confront another big stack late in the event, to slow down your betting decisions when you need to, to attack those short stacks, and so forth. Another valuable way to use a strategy card is to list your tournament goals for each stage of play as a reminder of why you are playing and what you expect to accomplish in each time period. Of course, the plan on your strategy card is not chiseled in stone; if it needs to be altered (maybe the lineup is different than you thought it would be), change it. Players who allow a predetermined strategy to rule their play, even though they know it is not working, lose tournaments. At the break, review your strategy card. Is it working for you right now, under these circumstances? Or should you change it?

## TIP 2: Rebuying and Adding On

The type of tournament you enter determines a major part of your playing strategy. For example, in freeze-out events, your primary concern in the early stages of play is making it to the next level in good shape. Therefore your strategy might be more conservative than it would be if you could replenish your chips with a timely rebuy if you went broke.

But most low-stakes tournaments are not freeze-outs: They allow multiple rebuys, either when you go broke or fall under a minimum chip status, plus an add-on at the end of the rebuy period. With all these opportunities for refilling your monetary canteen at the rebuy oasis, your strategy for traversing the occasional arid desert of tournament play will differ from freeze-out tourneys in which you cannot quench your thirst for chips except by winning them. The strategies in this book are geared to the popular rebuy and add-on events conducted by hundreds of cardrooms across the nation.

In most cases, you will need to take advantage of the rebuy and add-on options to be one of the top finishers. Therefore when you enter a rebuy tournament, take enough money to cover two or three rebuys and the add-on. For example, if the entry fee is $20, plan to spend $40 to $60 on the tournament (one or two $10 rebuys and the $10 add-on). If you are on a limited bankroll, it may be better to save your funds for a live action game or for a freeze-out event because your insufficient bankroll can become a significant drawback in playing optimal rebuy tournament strategy.

## When to Rebuy and Add On

When you go broke, it usually is correct to rebuy. If your winning expectation seems to be favorable — you feel confident that you can win and there will be a big payoff — rebuy so long as you feel comfortable with the number of times you do so. Although I have seen players make four or five rebuys, I believe that they probably should have accepted the decision of the poker gods who decided not to smile on them that day, and bow out of the fray. "Remember that the main reason you're playing the tournament is to get a big return on a small investment," T.J. Cloutier advises.

Deciding whether to add on usually is determined by your chip status when the add-on option comes up. If you are very low on chips, add on. If you are the chip leader, do not add on. And if you are in a middle chip position, it probably doesn't matter much one way or the other.

Who has the chips may also be a factor in deciding whether to add on, particularly in small tournaments (10 to 30 entrants) where you know most of the players. If you see that a very weak player who has been on a lucky streak holds one of the top chip positions, it probably is wise to take the add-on option so that you will have additional ammunition to use in taking advantage of his weak play. But if a strong player is top dog and you have a mid-sized stack, it probably will not increase your chances of a win enough to justify the add-on. If you are playing a tournament with a lot of entrants (more than 50 or so), most of whom you don't know, it is more difficult to determine the skill level of the players in top chip position. In that case, use your best judgment.

A mistake that chip leaders sometimes make is adding on unnecessarily. Many say that they buy the extra chips for insurance, but I suspect that the mental shadow of fear, their fear of losing the lead, also plays a part in their decision. Possibly the worst feeling I have ever experienced in a tournament is going to the final table as chip leader armed with my add-on insurance and finishing fourth in a three-way payout. "You choke when you get afraid and try to protect your lead," is the way Sykes put it.

Here are some additional pointers from the pros regarding rebuying. "If you're new to tournament play, forget it! Make it a one-shot deal," advised Sheahan, who believed that you should wait until you've had ample tournament experience before you decide to make major investments in them, and that you should "consider your single buy-in a fair price for the experience you gained."

Bobby Baldwin gives this advice: "Rebuy tournaments find many players with just enough money for the initial buy-in bucking up against well-heeled opponents who can gamble fast on marginal hands. The really inequitable danger comes from the highly-skilled cardsmiths with big bankrolls." If you find the competition just too tough for you to buck, back out in favor of entering a tourney with an easier lineup. Of course an easy lineup is becoming tougher to find because of the proliferation of tournaments across the world where you compete against the new breed of "tournament junkie."

Mike Caro advises adding on only if the add-on will build up your stack by a significant amount. "When in doubt, add on only if it will at least triple your chips." Obviously if you're very low on chips, the add-on is going to noticeably augment your stack, but if you already have a tower of chips, it won't add that much (what's one more turret when you already have six?) "When in doubt" probably best applies to those times when you're in a middle-stack status.

Michael Cappelletti expressed a different opinion of rebuy tournaments in an article he wrote for *Card Player*: "Rebuy tournaments are a psychological con device to get more money out of the players who otherwise might not put up a larger entry fee." (Freeze-out tournaments generally require about three times larger entry fees than rebuy events.) He further suggested that you play conservatively tight in a tournament that offers an add-on at a bargain price compared to the rebuy rate. (For example, you get 100 chips for a $10 rebuy, but 200 chips for a $10 add-on.) His reasoning for this conservative strategy is that it will save you "survival rebuys" at more expensive rates.

"Play as many hands as cheaply as you can if you're going to rebuy," Ron Limuti advised. "And decide in advance how much you're willing to invest in the tournament. If you play *right* from the start, you can reduce your rebuys."

Tom McEvoy adds this insight about rebuying: "I've been asked if it is always correct to rebuy when you go broke. My answer is no. The later you are in the rebuy period, the less reason you have to rebuy. The rebuy has less value to you at this stage because the limits are much higher."

## Incremental Rebuy Strategy

Some rebuy tournaments are structured so that when you rebuy, you get more chips for your money than you did for your entry fee. For example, suppose you paid a $120 entry fee and received $500 in chips to start, and you are allowed to make one rebuy and one add-on. For a $100 rebuy, you receive $800 in chips and for the $100 add-on, you receive $1,000 in chips. In this type of incremental rebuy structure, the rebuy and add-on strategy is different than when you receive the same number of chips for a rebuy as you did for your entry fee. Also, the amount of money that you should plan to invest in the tournament increases. McEvoy's advice on rebuying and adding on in incremental rebuy tournaments is this: "Basically, this type of event is telling you that although it only costs $120 to buy in, you should not play it if you aren't willing to invest $320 because you'll be taking so much the worst of it if you don't rebuy and add on. Plan to invest the maximum amount in incremental rebuy events."

As you can see from reading this section, your rebuy philosophy is an integral part of your tournament strategy.

## TIP 3: Play Assertively Early

Some tournament players have a tendency to play too tight, waiting for optimal starting hands to survive to the last table (although every tourney also seems to have its share of maniacs who try to run over you early-on). Although playing extra tight in the early rounds may be a viable strategy in no-rebuy tournaments, it is not an optimal strategy in rebuy events. (Of course, neither is playing too loosely.)

Some tight players are actually looking for an excuse to throw away their hands (yes!) perhaps to alleviate the stress of taking a big draw that may decimate their stacks. When a rock feels threatened by a big bad bettor (usually by the middle stages of the tourney), you can often take advantage of his timidity with bold, assertive play — running a bluff or trying a steal (easier to pull off in hold'em than in Omaha high-low). This style of play is called "playing fast."

The advantage of playing fast early in a tournament is that you can build a quantum stack to take into the later stages for a survival pad and for driving out the short stacks by intimidating them with strategic steals. The disadvantage is that you stand to lose all your chips and may need to rebuy several times.

Playing fast doesn't mean playing loose. Loose players enter pots with inferior or mediocre hands in the hope of hitting a flop with rags. Fast players come in with good hands, take the odds on their draws, and push their good hands to their fullest potential. When you play fast, you bet for value, raise, reraise — whatever you need to do — to build a pot that will pay you maximum value if you win it. You want to win as many chips *right now* as you can, realizing that you can play somewhat looser while the rebuy stage is still in effect. Your goal is to build a big stack for the later stages when you can no longer rebuy. You build that competitive stack with good hands and assertive play designed to squeeze out every drop of value — you do not do it with the maniac's reckless raises with wretched rags.

If the risk you take when you play fast appears to have a positive expectation, take it. But if the play-fast strategy isn't working for you, ease off and change gears. Maybe you're up against an opponent who's on a lucky streak, or several calling stations, or perhaps you're simply being out-played by a superior strategist. Or maybe you just aren't getting the cards you need to back up your assertive play.

The panel of pros has some solid advice on assertive fast play in the early stages of tournaments. "As to the actual playing style in the early stages — it's aggressive!" Sheahan said. He suggested raising with a live overcard in seven-card stud if you're in late position. Or calling an aggressive player's raise with a premium pair or a small live pair with a good kicker. "You'll either live fast or die young. Rocks seldom win this kind of play."

McEvoy notes that, "In the beginning stages of a fast-action tournament (one with short betting rounds), players often tend to play too fast, especially in the smaller tournaments with a buy-in range from $25 to $45 with rebuys for the first hour." He suggests that you play more conservatively than they do if you don't plan to rebuy. My observations of low-limit tournament players verify what Tom is saying — many don't draw a line between loose and fast, and a lot of them seem to put no limit on the number of rebuys they are willing to make to compensate for their loose play. I hate playing against these maniacs because it is very hard to put them on a hand, although if they survive to the later stages, they can become major contributors to your wealth.

On the flip side, if making multiple rebuys is part of your strategy, you can loosen up your starting requirements. "You might take a slightly inferior hand in Texas hold'em, like 8-7 suited, and gamble with it (in a multiway pot)," McEvoy suggests. "It's likely there are big pairs or big cards out against you, which means that the deck should be rich in middle-value cards." Remember that more pots are played multiway in the early stages than in the middle stage, and certainly far more than in the late stage when most pots are played either heads-up or three-way.

There is more than one theory about how to play in a tournament's early stages. Some players push on the "Charge!" button and never turn it off. Others think that you just have to make the most of the cards you're dealt, while being assertive with them. Some rocks sit and wait for the nuts like squirrels. "If you play a Joe Conservative style, forget it!" advised Sheahan. "Your checks will melt away like icicles in July." Choose a style that is right for you — probably neither squeaky tight nor super aggressive will do the trick.

McEvoy believes that "solid aggressive" is the optimal tournament style: "Solid aggressive is the way I describe my own style. I throw away a lot of hands but when I'm in a pot, I try to take the lead. Good judgment and knowledge of your opponents' play also are essential for success."

## TIP 4: Play Straightforward Poker

The value of deception decreases in tournament play, especially during the early to middle stages. Slow-playing a big hand sometimes costs much more than the extra bets you would ordinarily hope to gain from this ring-game strategy. One of the reasons for this is because the population at your tournament table is ever changing as players drop out and others are transferred in from other tables. There is an inverse ratio between deceptive value and the number of times players change in your ring. Therefore you usually are better off to simply play your hand straightforwardly.

Here is an example from an Omaha high-low tourney that illustrates this point. Small Blind held 10-

10-8-7 and protected his blind by calling the unraised pot before the flop. He was happy to see the flop come 10-3-3, making him the nut full house. He checked to his two opponents with the intention of zapping them with a check-raise, but neither one bet.

When a jack came on the turn, Small Blind bet out — this time, both players called. He put one of them on a J-3 and the other on a possible A-3 or 10-3. The river washed up flotsam for Small Blind: a red queen. When he bet his full house, Opponent Two raised. Calling the raise with a premonition of doom, Big Blind saw his house get sucked up and blown away by a queens-full tornado. Because no one had bet on the flop, Opponent Two needed to call only one bet to see his miracle card fall on the river and promote his A-4-Q-Q to the nuts. (Actually, not quite the nuts — if another three had come on the river, Player Two would have won it with his A-3-8-9!)

"Slow-playing of solid hands is not necessary in tournaments because the pace is fast," Sheahan advised. The only time you may want to slow-play a big hand in Omaha high-low is when you make quads with three of your rank on the board. Or in Texas hold'em when you flop the nut full house. In these rare instances, you may receive more value from checking than from betting, because someone with a good pocket pair often will bet his overpair or second-nut full house on the turn. You can then call and, if you are positioned *after* him, raise on the river. If you are in front of him, bet out rather than try a check-raise on the river because your opponent may not bet his second-nut full house or overpair again.

In a seven-card stud tournament that I entered when I was a novice tournament player, I held rolled-up sevens (two hidden sevens with a third seven on top) against two competitors in the late stages of the tourney. Deciding to slow-play, I just called the bring-in bet. The lady on my left raised. "How nice of her to raise my pot for me!" I thought to myself. Taking it to the river with various raising-calling tactics, I was staring down the throat of her ace-high flush with no improvement for my set of sevens.

In retrospect, I think that I should have reraised my opponent's raise (which she made on the strength of three flush cards to the ace), but I got greedy and slow-played the hand, forgetting that "a pot in the hand is worth two in the bush" or something like that. (But hey, I won the tournament and she came in third, thanks to the chips she yanked out of my slow-playing pocket!)

Losing the power of deceptive moves such as slow-playing, having to gauge his play by his stack size, and often being forced into survival strategies are three reasons why an aggressive buddy of mine does not compete in tourneys. "Tournaments just don't fit my style," he explained. "It's like being tied up in a straightjacket." Mason Malmuth doesn't like to play in tourneys, either. "One reason is that I don't particularly like to sit for a long period of time. Another is that some of the survival strategies, which at times are correct in poker tournaments, run counter to the way I want to gamble." To my way of thinking, both men are missing a major part of modern poker action as tournaments become increasingly more popular and profitable.

If you enjoy the challenge of intense competition at an escalating pace, and if you are willing to adjust your ring-game strategy by using the 20 tournament techniques in this book, you may find that you *prefer* tournament action to regular play. And with practice, patience and expertise, you may win a ton of trophies and lot of loot (plus some bragging rights).

# TIP 5: Keep Track of Your Stack

Always be aware of your stack's relative status and your playing position at the table. For example, if you have a very low stack in hold'em with an average hand and are sitting in a middle position, be inclined to throw away your cards. Save your chips in the hope of catching a stronger hand in a later, more favorable position.

Suppose you are in the big blind in a hold'em event and have only enough money left for the small blind and perhaps two extra bets. A player three seats to your left also is on a short stack with only enough chips to meet the blinds plus one more bet. If someone raises, you may not want to call the raise (defend your blind), but instead allow the other short stack the opportunity to either go all in before he gets to the blinds or be blinded out.

When you are in strong chip status and good position, you can attack the blinds with a raise if you have a playable hand and they are low on chips, especially if they are very tight. If they fold, you own their chips. If they call, you have the positional advantage to raise them all-in with a favorable flop and possibly eliminate them from the tournament.

But if you are in good chip status and so is the player to your left, allow him to attack the blinds (provided he is aggressive), thus preserving your own stack. It is the "duty" of either you or him to try to get the blinds out of the game if either if them is very low on chips (if you have a playable hand). Taking out a late competitor is usually a one-man job.

If you are the tournament leader, try to eliminate the weak spots as soon as you can and as often as you can in order to reduce the competition and increase your chances of winning. I recall a tournament in which one of the more experienced players complained because a timid opponent with a tall stack piled in front of him did not take out a short stack when he had the chance. It was a justified complaint: That short stack rebuilt himself and took third place.

## TIP 6: Become a Speed Reader

Tournament action is fast. In typical low-stakes limit events, the betting increments rise every 15 to 20 or 30 minutes. Someone seems to blow himself out of the competition just about every time the increments increase, causing a player to be transferred to the empty seat and changing the composition and nature of the table. So putting players on hands and reading tells — *quickly* — becomes very important to your tournament survival.

If the only hand you're playing is the one that you are holding, prepare for a quick exit from action. Staying mentally alert and observing the play of your opponents, especially the better players, are only two facets of speed-reading. Chapter Seven shows you several more.

## TIP 7: Take Advantage of Tight Opponents

Big bets are like thermometers that measure the looseness-tightness of many tournaments. As the betting increments increase, the tightness of most competitors also increases. Although rocks don't realize it, tightening up like a rusty bottle cap that you can't twist off a brew is anti-productive to winning. This is not to say that you should not play tight — just that playing *nut*-tight doesn't usually get the money.

You can take advantage of too-tight players by entering the pot with a somewhat more marginal hand if you are in a late position and no one has yet opened the pot. But be more cautious when a tight-timid player has entered the action in front of you because the chances are that he's holding a strong hand. If you are in your fast mode, you can raise with a calling hand to discourage tight-timid opponents who are sitting behind you from calling the pot.

Judging from my low-limit tournament experience, many competitors play too loose in the early stages and too tight in the later stages — they have it reversed. By playing *loose* in the early betting rounds (which many of them misinterpret as playing fast), they often are forced to rebuy more frequently. Then when they begin playing tight in the late stages, they forfeit opportunities to steal uncontested pots.

The trick is to appear to be a tight player but to actually play more liberally than your opponents think you do. Your tight image gives you a strong front from which you can run an occasional steal, especially in the late stages. It takes more courage for most players to call a bet than it does to make a bet, and it often takes a lot more bravery to call a tight player. So if your image is tight (ideally, tight-aggressive), take advantage of it by occasionally running over the tight-timids in late play.

## TIP 8: Change Gears

Playing a tournament reminds me of driving my first car, a lime green 1961 stick-shift VW bug with four gears. Sometimes you have to shift into second to speedup the pace of your game while you sometimes have to slow down until the maniacs get off the shoulders. And every now and then, you have to put on the brakes. The trick is knowing when to shift.

In poker tournaments, you need to develop a sixth sense for when to shift gears, that is change the pace, strategy or style of your play. And you've got to do it quickly because game conditions can change as fast as the weather on the Mojave Desert. Sheahan suggested that you change gears when you have a big stack in the late stages of a tournament by "abandoning the aggressive style of play that probably got you there." At this point in the action, you move into a more conservative mode by throwing away marginal hands and allowing other players to pick each other off. Don't let your big stack's power get siphoned away by making calls with marginal cards.

Another time you should consider changing gears is in the opening stages of a tourney if playing fast isn't working for you. Lean back and slow down. Wait for better cards and then shift back into your fast gear when you start catching better hands.

Advanced players can confuse their opponents when they change gears to speed up the action. Many novice tournament players cannot keep up with betting action that is fast (continual raises and reraises). Pros know how to use this to their advantage. As Brunson said, "Aggressive poker puts fear in your opponents, it wins the chips, and it feeds your competitive instincts like nothing else."

Even betting with very fast hand movements can confuse slower or more tentative competitors, intimidating them into backing off, possibly with the best hand, from what they perceive as dangerous aggression. If an aggressive player is trying to hurry your decisions with either quick betting or vocal intimidation ("We haven't got all day, fella!"), you can change *his* gears by slowing all of your betting movements. Make him wait. Try his patience. Control his (e)motions. Shift into reverse: if he bets fast, you bet slow. If he bets slow, you bet fast. This is a ploy that supersalesmen often use to manipulate the decisions of a potential buyer — if the buyer is speaking fast and slinging out multiple objections to his product, a sharp salesman will slow things down, hear him out, and then quietly and slowly answer each of his objections to the sale.

Another important time to slow down is when you are low on chips in the later stages of the tournament. The survival techniques discussed in Chapter Five are designed to help you weather the roadblocks of survival to the final table.

Tournaments require that you change gears to win. Work this concept into your Strategy Card. In the early rounds, you can drive faster than on the final laps when you probably will be slowing your speed. During the middle rounds, you sometimes will be playing fast and other times will shift into your survival mode, something like taking the yellow flag at the Indy 500. If you drive full-bore through a tournament doing 85 m.p.h. all the way, you may wind up someplace you didn't want to be — on the rail rather than in the winners' circle.

# TIP 9: Watch the Clock

Good tournament strategists watch their stacks, the other players *and* the clock. Think of the tournament as a pie that is divided into as many pieces as there are time periods. Within each piece of the tournament pie, there are somewhat definable sequences of action. In Texas hold'em you probably will face the blinds only twice during a 20-minute round. In Omaha high-low, you probably will play the blinds only once during a short round because of the split nature of most pots.

You sometimes need to time your moves according to the movement of the clock's hands. For example, your goal may be to increase your stack by 50 percent during each round. Looking at your watch, you realize that the time is almost over in the round. You're in late position and so you decide to play a reasonable hand faster than you normally would play it. Why? Because the betting limits will double within the next two hands. You can take this opportunity to try to increase your stack size while the bets are still at the less-expensive rate. Experienced tournament players often use this ploy. (Don't feel pressured, however, into playing a very marginal hand under the time-pressure gun.)

Tournament winner Norm Michaud added, "The relationship between time and chips is a constant factor in every decision. If it's late in the time period and the cards just aren't coming, I know I'll have to wait it out for now, but I'll want to be more aggressive early in the next betting round." Therefore another opportune time to play more aggressively than usual is at the beginning of the higher-limit round. I think this is particularly true when the bets double every round rather than rise more slowly. "It's $50-$100 now," your opponents may think, "so I'd better be twice as careful."

Of course, also be aware of the stage of the tournament (early, middle, late). For example, if you have a short stack in the middle stage of a fast-action tournament (short betting rounds of 15 to 20 minutes), McEvoy suggests that "You have to double up. Double up or get up! You don't have to wait for a premium hand, so play that king-jack (in hold'em) with a raise, even from up front. Chances are you won't get any better cards in this round anyway."

Or if you are in short stack status on the last hand before the final add-on, you may want to throw in those extra chips with a good, playable holding. This is advisable because all the lower-denomination chips usually are raced off the table on the first hand after the add-on option is over, giving you added value for your auction-block chips if you win the hand.

In general, two good times to play fast or to bet aggressively are just before the increments increase to make full use of your chips at the current lower price, and just after the bets rise to take advantage of opponents who may be fearful of the higher stakes. As Sykes advised me, "If you can win one pot at each increment, you can sustain yourself." And more often than not, winning just one pot per level will be enough to take you to the championship table.

## TIP 10: Practice, Practice!

Before you decide to enter a tournament with a big buy-in (say $200 -$1,000), play in as many small buy-in tourneys as you can find. In general, as the buy-in increases, so does the sophistication of the players. Although the number of entries often is smaller, the competition usually is stiffer in higher buy-in tournaments than it is in low buy-in tourneys, so get some mileage under your belt before you tackle the big boys. You can do this by beginning your tournament career in lower buy-in tourneys, gradually progressing through the medium ranks until you have enough expertise to compete against the best players for the highest stakes.

Another way to practice is to get on the rail at some high stakes tournaments and observe how people play. Take notes. Did they make some moves you can use in your next event? Are they doing things differently from the way players do them in low-limit tournaments? What? How? *Why*?

Baldwin suggested another way to increase your competence: "Young, dedicated students of poker, after a reasonable period of exposure to educational reading, can tear up ordinary players who have used experience as their only teacher." As a professional writer, I am attracted to Baldwin's suggestion. You must be too, or you wouldn't have invested in this book. I believe that I have saved far more money from the valuable ideas I have learned in poker books than I paid for them (and I've read them *all*). Books are much less expensive teachers than experience alone. When a loser tells you, "I'm paying for my lessons," you can believe that he's paying far too expensive a price for tutelage at the tables.

My final suggestion is to stage a mental rehearsal before you make your grand entry onto the tournament stage. To build your self-confidence before you enter any event, mentally prepare yourself by designing your strategy, memorizing it, and affirming to yourself that you are capable of winning. Caro's famous affirmation is: "I am a lucky player. A powerful winning force surrounds me." If it's good enough for Mike, it's surely good enough for me!

Believe you are a winner. See yourself raking in all the chips and counting the wads of $100-bills that you have won. Imagine carrying home an impressive trophy and celebrating your glorious moment of victory with family and friends. "What the mind of man can perceive and believe, it can achieve." Napoleon Hill (*Think and Grow Rich*).

*A player who is only tight has little chance of scoring a big win unless the cards run all over him. A player who is only loose has little chance of winning anything. Play solid. A solid player is a skillful player who sometimes plays tight and sometimes plays loose. And of course, always play happy.*

**— Roy West**

# CHAPTER 5

# 11 MORE TOURNAMENT TIPS

♦

My grandfather would rather have folded aces-full than make a list with only 10 items on it, so here are more tactics that you can use to destroy the competition in your next tournament. Along with the first 10 tips, they are just about all you will need to win your next 100 low-limit tournaments.

## Tip 11: Survival Techniques

Big Al was sitting on the button with the J♥ 10♥, a medium stack, and three opponents in the late stages of a hold'em tournament. The flop came A♦ 9♥ 8♥. Opponent One bet, Number Two called, Number Three folded, and Big Al called. The turn produced the 2♣. Again Opponent One bet and again Number Two called. So did Al. On the river came Al's straight card, the 7♣, and he raked in a nice pot.

"I've seen you play lotsa poker," his buddy Bob chided from the rail, "but I ain't never seen you play like a pussy cat before," referring to Big Al's just calling with his straight-flush draw rather than playing it fast. Big Al's retort cannot be reproduced in this learned tome. Suffice to say that he did not appreciate Bob's appraisal of his tournament play, which was different from his ring-game style. In a cash game, Big (aggressive) Al would have raised on the flop to add value to his straight and flush draws. If his raise didn't buy him a free card on the turn, he would have raised any player who bet into him.

But this was a tournament and his chip tank was running out of gas. Al suspected that Opponent One probably held a big ace (an ace with a king or queen kicker) or aces up, and he thought that Opponent Two might have a higher flush draw than his own. Further, Al had only two opponents to build a pot for his possible win. Since it was late in the tournament, Big Al didn't want to take unnecessary chances with his drawing hand in case he didn't make it on the end.

Whether you agree with Al's strategy in the play of this hand — and there are some of you who probably think that Al's friend was right about him — this is an example of playing "survival poker" in real tournament action. If Al's big draw had not materialized, he believed that he would be unable to survive to the last table. Therefore he chose not to put himself in jeopardy by betting his drawing hand for full value, preferring to take a reasonable profit if he made the hand rather than risking being eliminated if he lost it.

Survival does not mean that you should play super tight and timid poker. What it does mean is that you won't be playing as many marginal hands and you won't be betting your drawing hands for maximum value. Players usually go into survival mode later in the tournament when they cannot rebuy, when they are low on chips, when they aren't catching playable hands, and sometimes even when they want to protect a big stack. They survive by using some of these tactics:

## Avoid late confrontations with big stacks

Even if your stack is equal to the other major contender for the pot, do not enter the fray if your hand is marginal. Wait for better cards. At this point in the action, you want to minimize your risk of losing ground in the chip standings. One way that you do this is by minimizing the number of hands you play that require a lucky flop to win. You would prefer going in with hands that can win the pot outright if the flop falls with blanks, rather than a hand that requires a draw.

## Wait as long as you can for a playable hand

"If you're not catching any cards, you just have to wait," advises McEvoy. He also suggests that, if you don't make your hand on the flop when you're in survival mode, you should immediately muck it to save enough chips for another outing with Lady Luck. He also advises players to always remember that the smaller the pot, the less reason you have to enter it, especially with a drawing hand.

## Don't play hands that require a big draw to win

Be more inclined to enter the pot with hands that have pot-winning potential on the flop. You may not be able to stretch your chips far enough to take the draw you need to make the hand, because calling a bet or a raise would put you all-in and eliminate you from contention if you don't get any help on the turn or river.

Also there is a good chance that you won't get full value on your hand even if you do make it, particularly if it is late in the tournament, because most competitors play tighter in the late stages and will not call you anyway. Because more hands are played heads-up or three-way (rather than multiway) in the late stage, you usually will not be getting proper odds on your drawing hands. Strong players who flop a big hand will make it very expensive for you to draw. They want to shut you out and win the pot *right now* without giving you a chance to outdraw them on the next betting round.

## Don't be overly aggressive

If you have a short stack in survival mode, you usually cannot afford to make a play at the pot unless you have a premium hand. Above all, try to save enough chips to see one more hand — don't throw in your extras when you do not flop to your hand.

With a big stack in survival mode, you can protect your standing by playing very solid poker. Don't jeopardize your top-dog status with hot-dog moves, the types of plays that Caro refers to as "the fancy play syndrome." Conservative play balanced with stable thinking is the winning ticket in survival mode. "You must master the science of inconspicuous survival," Caro further advises.

Not everybody agrees that you should go into a survival cocoon. Counter to this strategy is Bob Ciaffone's advice: "You must make a lot of money on your good starting hands to win a tournament. Don't play *survivalist poker*. For most tournament payoff structures, it takes about 20 ninth-place finishes to make as much money as winning one tournament. Go for the gold!" (Some low-limit tourneys award only a free buy-in to ninth place while the winner gets a payout of $600-$1,000.) In the short run, you have to decide what will work best for you in your long run for that gold.

## TIP 12: Play Smart Late

In the late stages, whether a play is smart depends on four things: the strength of your hand, your comparative chip status, the nature of your opponents, and your attitude about whether it is better to play conservatively just to get to the last table, even with a low stack, or whether it is better to gamble with a low or medium stack in an attempt to build up your chips for the final conquest.

Some tournament players prefer being aggressive with a short stack, particularly at the second-to-last table, because they believe that they will need a bigger cushion of chips to have a chance at winning the event. Other players prefer simply getting to the final table, regardless of chip status, and therefore they usually will not play as aggressively as they would if they had a plumper chip cushion. It's a close call, but in very low-limit events ($10-$20 buy-in) I believe that it is better to try to build up your stack by putting a little more gamble into your play. Why? Because most of the real money to be won will be awarded to the top three finishers.

Most tournament players would agree that a big stack is worth protecting. Beginners often make the mistake of playing more hands than they should with a monster stack, no matter what stage of the tourney they are in. However once you have a mountain of chips, you want to protect it with solid play, rather than allowing it to erode into a molehill by betting marginal hands and loosening up your play more than table conditions warrant.

Always remember that the real win in any tournament is centered in the top three payout spots. Several strategies will help you get there. One of them is avoiding major confrontations with another big stack whenever you can. You would rather get the small stacks out of action than risk your chip position by going up against an opponent who is just as strong as you are, so you play more aggressively against short stacks and tighter against big stacks. Another thing to remember is not to squander big chips on little hands. Play *very* smart with a monster stack late in the tournament.

Medium stacks probably are the most difficult to play. With a middle stack, your goal in the later stages of the tournament is to build your stack, survive the cut and come in for the money. Playing smart-late means not playing marginal hands, not pushing the edges, and not raising for maximum value on drawing hands (if you play them at all) that could break you if you don't make your hand.

When you are on the short end of the stick with the hungry blinds moving in fast to gobble up the tiny morsel of chips you have left, you may be best advised to take McEvoy's advice: "You can't wait for the nuts or even a big hand. You have to take a shot with any playable hand and be aggressive with it." He thinks that it is best to get all your chips in early in the betting if you have only enough left to play one hand. You either win the pot outright or you may make the best hand on the river. The idea is to force out marginal hands that may have beaten you if you hadn't raised coming in.

Let me illustrate some not-too-smart late play. As a beginner, I was near the top in chip status at the final table of an Omaha high-low tournament. The blind was all-in on the first hand of the first betting round, and recalling that one of the "duties" of a big stack is to take out the short stacks, I raised with an A-A-9-8 double-suited from first position. Naturally I didn't expect either of the other two big stacks to call — surely they knew I had a "mission" to complete -- but one of them did. And I'll never forget her.

The flop came with two low cards in my suit and an offsuit nine, giving me top board pair, the nut-flush draw, a weak low draw, an inside-straight draw and a premium overpair. Feeling pretty confident, I bet. The Lady called. The turn card was a lowly six. When I bet again, The Lady raised. Now I was in a bind, having only enough chips to call three-fourths of her raise for an all-in stand — or fold and be reduced to low-stack status with the big blind fast approaching. I called all-in. A river ace gave me trip aces. When she exposed her cards, I stared in disbelief at the axe that had chopped down my double-suited aces: an unsuited 2-3-4-5, giving The Lady not only a wheel but a six-high straight.

I had committed the ultimate late-stage tournament mistake: pitting myself against a player who had better position, an equal stack *and* cards that fit the flop perfectly. Dragging my weary body from the table, I soothed my pain with a roll of quarters and a vengeful attack on a video-poker machine.

# TIP 13: When You're In the Late Lead

When you are in a strong chip position late in a tourney, you may be wise to call more often than you normally would, especially in late position against short stacks. Even if you think that you may be a slight underdog, call anyway, particularly heads-up. Sometimes a small stack can rebuild itself by just winning the antes or blinds, which may help him considerably. The small bet you must call will not hurt you that much, and it could help you a lot if the short stack misses and is eliminated.

Of course, use your common sense and your knowledge of the strength of your opponents whenever you call. You don't want your strong chip position to be washed away by an ocean of loose or careless calls, so you make only carefully considered, positional calls.

## TIP 14: Avoid Big Confrontations

Imagine this scenario at the final table: Small Blind has a tall stack, Big Blind has a medium stack of chips, and Aggressor is sitting on the button with Mount Everest. Aggressor raises and Small Blind reraises. Seeing a big confrontation ready to come down between the hold'em tournament leaders, Big Blind folds his pair of tens and sits back to observe the ensuing battle.

Why would Big Blind dump a pair of tens in late three-way action? Because he thinks that one of the tall stacks may knock the other big stack low enough to allow him to sneak into second-place money. In that case, he would become the biggest winner of the pot. Of course, if Big Blind had been very low on chips, he would have put them all in: If you're in weak chip status with a good hand, you don't care how big the other guy's stack is.

If survival is your foremost consideration late in a tournament, you usually should not pit your big stack against an opponent who is equally strong, or who could take over the lead with a favorable flop. If you are going to confront someone, try to choose a player with a short stack. If they're helpless, down to the last few pennies they have left in life, attack! But to stay alive, you must first survive, so attack *selectively*.

## TIP 15: Late Stage, Big Stack

"If they're playing tight, you play fast. If they're gambling recklessly, then you do the opposite — lay back and play only premium hands," McEvoy advises. He also suggests that you should play mostly against the short stacks and try to run over as many blinds as you can. Although a tall stack gives you more latitude in your moves late in a tournament, still you cannot afford to sit through *Gone With The Wind* waiting for a playable hand.

If the short stacks decide to gamble with you, give action with your solid hands, but fold marginal ones. "With anything playable, you're forced to gamble if the short stacks begin to get aggressive, because a lot of the time they'll decide that they have nothing to lose," McEvoy notes. Because of the rapidly escalating blinds or antes, you cannot afford to allow an aggressive player to continually steal from you. With all that chicken feed to fatten his stacks, he may soon become as fat a cat as you are.

If the short stacks are not being aggressive and you've built an Eiffel Tower of chips, still play only premium hands as much as you can. Be alert to the dangers of "tower thinking" in which a chip leader squanders part (or all) of a big stack by playing too aggressively or entering too many pots. Instead be grateful for a lull in action that gives you time to wait for a premium holding with which to defend your fortress.

If you and another opponent have tall stacks of about the same size with a third player hanging on with a short stack, play your strong hands somewhat more conservatively than you usually would. You don't want to jeopardize your chances of making the final two or three. McEvoy's reasoning is that it is better to be cautious than to get trapped for extra bets that might promote the strength of the short stack. The Bermuda Triangle is not a pleasant place to get stranded.

## TIP 16: Late Stage, Short Stack

Playing a short stack in the late stages of a tournament is a tricky proposition. If you are within striking range of the final table, is it better to be aggressive and go for the gold to build a competitive stack for your final table attack? Or is it best to shift into survival in an attempt to arrive there with any number of chips you can manage?

Baldwin suggests a money management technique for this situation that he calls "coasting," which he sees as "a compromise with defeat." Just the opposite of the maniacs who throw both caution and chips to the wind, coasting is a viable alternative to risking everything. "Somewhere between these two are the rare *control* players who usually win," he advises.

What do these control players do to assure survival? They wait as long as they can for a playable hand because it takes a comparatively stronger hand to enter a pot with a short stack. They are very conservative about getting into major confrontations with anybody. Rather than going all in with their "leftover" chips, control players hang on to them as though they were bars of solid gold in the hope that a chip and a chair will ensure them at least a payout in the tournament money.

When you are extremely low on chips at the final table, you are a target for the chip hunters who zero in on the bulls-eye they see painted on your forehead. You must control your emotions (although you'd rather be able to control the cards) and play your very best poker. But there comes a time when you have to take a stand because the blinds and antes will eat up your chips faster than kids munch Fritos — whether or not you play a hand. "At this point, cornered solid players will play almost any marginal hand aggressively," advised Sheahan. "Remember that you are gambling and it usually is better to go down shooting!"

Next time you're at the final table with only two chips and the blinds fast approaching, remember that many tournament winners survived similar situations. At the 1982 World Series of Poker, Jack Straus was groveling in the chip trenches with only one bullet left in his tournament gun. By the time he arrived at the final table, he had built that one chip into over one-half the chips on the table — and went on to win the title!

## TIP 17: Late Stage, Medium Stack

Having a midsize stack in the late stages of the tournament is something like being the middle child in a family of three: The older kid gets the privileges and the younger one gets the attention. All you get is the kitchen chores. While Tall Stack enjoys the luxury of waiting for a big hand to pick off Short Stack, Middle Marvin is left with the challenge of either moving up the ladder or getting pushed further down it.

If you are too aggressive with a mid-stack in the late stages, you may soon join Short Stack, even though your intent is to topple Tall Stack. If you're too passive, you don't have the chance of a snowball in Death Valley. So what is your best strategy? Selective aggression sprinkled with survivalism — as in a shorthanded pot that no one has bet. As Bob Ciaffone wrote, "There are a lot of tournament pots that have a 'For Sale' sign on them. You may be the only person willing to risk any money. All top tournament players are quick to bet the flop in shorthanded pots."

Of course, your strategy will be determined in part by how your opponents are playing. Are the big stacks laying back, playing conservatively so that they can get to the last table in good shape? If so, you probably can play more aggressively against them. Are the short stacks becoming impatient, playing looser in a last-ditch run for the brass ring? You'll probably need to stay out of their way and let Tall Stack knock them off in the hope of promoting your standing a notch or two. But if Short Stack is playing very conservative poker, you can come at him yourself in the hope of piling his chips on top of yours to better position yourself to make a run at Tall Stack later on.

Your goal is to get to that final table. If you see your chips diminishing to the danger level, play very patient poker. Wait as long as you can for a playable hand and then bet it for as much value as you can without endangering yourself. In survival mode, you are more concerned about making the last table than with squeezing every drop of value from your good hands. It is one way of buying insurance, like you do in blackjack. If your A-K gets clobbered by a low set, you'll still have one bet left for the next deal.

Play conservatively, though not timidly. You don't want the big stacks to perceive you as a pushover and start scrambling to rake off your chips. It is better to have them think that you are capable of playing with them so that they don't continually try to steal from you. Without jeopardizing your survival in the event, try to set up one more winning hand or two so that you can make it to the final table with enough chips to be competitive. It is a very thin line to tread.

## TIP 18: Very Late? Don't Wait!

As players are eliminated and fewer players enter pots, it usually takes less strength to win a pot. Many beginners find it hard to grasp that you don't always need a premium hand to win a big-money pot in the final stages of tournament play. This happens for several reasons: People are entering fewer pots because they are in survival mode; some are playing scared because they are afraid of losing and will not take a reasonable gamble; and many pots are played shorthanded, which requires a different set of skills than full-ring poker. It is these shorthanded pots that often have the "For Sale" sign on them that Ciaffone referred to. (I heartily recommend that you study and practice shorthanded strategies to increase your chances of winning at the final table.)

In Omaha high-low, it is not unusual for high pair or third-nut low to win all or half the pot in the final tournament stages. A pair of sixes won the final pot in a tourney I entered that had an $1,100 payout for first place. (Unfortunately, the sixes were not in my hand.) In seven-card stud, one good pair often does the trick, and that pair usually wins before seventh street because players are not as willing to take a draw in a game that has five betting rounds. Second-best pair in Texas hold'em often is good enough to win a pot and any hand with an ace in it probably is playable in the extremely late stage. In fact when you are playing heads-up at the final table, Cloutier points out that, "You don't need as strong a starting hand to get involved with. Any ace is super powerful. Pocket pairs that are eights or higher also are strong." What you are looking for is a hand that can take the pot without a showdown. This is not the hour of power for drawing hands and, of course, rags are never correct to play.

I once folded two pair against three betting-and-calling opponents in the final stages of an Omaha high-low event. With both a flush and a straight possible on the river, my two-pair seemed doomed to defeat and so I folded the hand. I was dumbfounded to see a pair of nines take the high end of the pot and an A-7 come in for low. I added making that end call with a medium stack in late position to my list of "Things I Wish I'd Done." And I vowed to remember that it is only a minor loss when you make a losing call that costs you just one bet — but it is a disaster to *not* make a call that would have won you the pot.

## TIP 19: Bluff Against Weakness

Bluffing plays a definite role in tournament strategy, though probably not as big a part as some novices imagine. Actually it is tougher to run a successful bluff in limit hold'em than it is in no-limit hold'em because so many players have a "river" mentality, something like, "Be there or be square." Three things to consider when you decide to bluff include:

- ♠ Who should you bluff?
- ♠ When can you bluff?
- ♠ What type of bluff should you use?
- ♠ What type of player can you bluff?

The primary goal of a good tournament bluff is to win the pot immediately. Another aim is to limit the field. Bluffs are best executed by players who have tall stacks and are perceived to be playing tightly. The best bluffs are always against weakness: a tight-timid player, one in a weak table position, or a player with a short stack and a weak heart.

The timing of a tournament bluff is very important. In the beginning stages of rebuy events, almost everyone is playing looser than they intend to play later on. In the later stages, many people are playing tighter than they need to. It is easier to bluff a tight opponent than a loose one because tight players will lay down a hand when they figure they're beaten, but a loose player will almost always go for the draw. Saving most of your bluffs for the later stages when players have "nutted up" is a good guideline to follow.

Bluffing, then, becomes more profitable after the rebuy period is over, and the closer you are to the final table. During these later stages when many players are hibernating in their survival cocoons, you can take advantage of their tight play with a well-timed bluff. If a player's stack is low and his backbone is weak, attack him with a big stack, a mid-stack, any stack. He is your most vulnerable target.

Be aware of the stack status and the tight-loose index of a player before you try to bluff him. Also count how many players are yet to act after you. For example, if a rock is low on chips and you are both in a late position with only one other opponent between the two of you, go for it. Rocks are easier to bluff than any other type of player because they will lay down a lot of hands that others will call with.

Two players that you do not want to tangle with on a bluff move are Tall Stack and Loose Goose. If you hold a low or mid-sized stack, Tall Stack may sense that you are making a move and will call you with even a marginal hand because he figures that he has less to lose than you do. Seasoned players know that it is far more difficult to bluff Loose Goose than someone who is either tight or is at least reasonable.

If you have a short stack, trying to bluff probably is suicidal. Usually, the shorter your stack, the stronger the hand you must hold to enter a late pot. No matter what your stack size, it usually is best not to try to bluff a tall stack, especially one who is both perceptive and aggressive.

Some less experienced players have but one type of bluff in their repertoires, the end bluff, but more skillful cardsmiths also use the semibluff from a front position with, for example, second-best pair in hold'em to try to steal the pot outright. You can also use the bluff-raise in later positions to find out how strong the original bettor's hand really is or to steal the pot outright. If he reraises, which he may do with either a strong hand or as a defensive move (the bluff reraise), you can lay down the hand without further investment.

In a multiway pot with strong chip position, you may consider the come-bluff when you hold something such as four to a flush or straight. This maneuver is better made in the beginning stages when people usually are playing looser and more players are in each pot, thus increasing your payoff if you win the pot. But when things tighten up in the later stages, the come-bluff is not as appropriate for two reasons. First, callers will have better hands than they played earlier. Second, fewer people will call because most opponents play tighter late in the tourney, thus reducing your chances of getting full value for a hand even if you make it.

It is easier to bluff when there are *scare* cards on the flop in Texas hold'em or on the board in seven-card stud. The following scenario occurred during the middle stages of a low-limit hold'em tournament: Big Blind was all-in before the flop. Player Two called from first position with the J♦ 10 ♥. Small Blind called the pot with a mid-sized stack. The flop came down with 9♠ 8♠ Q♦ which gave Player Two the nut straight. When Small Blind bet into her, Player Two raised and Small Blind called the raise.

On the turn came the 6♠. Small Blind checked, Player Two bet her straight and Small Blind just called, making quite a nice side pot between the two (the Big Blind was in for only the main pot). The river card was a real shocker to Player Two: the 2♠, making four spades on the board. This time Small Blind bet first and Player Two folded to what she thought must be Small Blind's spade flush.

Of course, Small Blind had to expose his hand to Big Blind in order to win the main pot. A pair of nines! Having no spade to complete the four-card board flush and only a pair of sixes, the Big Blind conceded the pot to the Small Blind's well-timed front bluff on the river. (Player Two vowed to have her brother-in-law repossess Small Blind's new Camaro!)

## Tip 20: Learn to Fold When You Know You Should

Making correct laydowns (folds) is a point that McEvoy emphasizes in *Tournament Poker*: "Getting married to a hand is one of the biggest mistakes that tournament players make. Making proper laydowns is essential to your success because you cannot replenish those precious chips (after the rebuy period is over) once you lose them." Many players accustomed to playing only ring games often continue with a hand much longer than they should. They don't realize that the hand requirements that people set for themselves in tournaments often are higher than they are in cash games. "A hand that might be playable in a ring game often is far more dangerous to play in a tournament," Cloutier said in *Championship Hold'em*.

It takes discipline, the self-control that Baldwin talked about, to master the temptation to call when, down deep inside, you know that you should fold. As Cloutier put it, "Making the correct laydowns in the right situations separates the winners from the losers. Winners realize that it is critical in tournaments to get away from hands that they may very well continue playing in ring games. This requires discipline."

Top tournament players have no more trouble with folding than they do with raising. For example, at the final table of the no-limit hold'em championship event at the 1999 Tournament of Champions, winner David Chiu actually folded pocket kings before the flop when Louis Asmo, who finished second, raised all in.

Graciously, Asmo showed the gallery his pocket aces after Chiu had folded.

"If your hand is beat, it's beat and there's nothing you can do about it except to fold as early as possible. Sometimes saving only one or two bets with a prudent laydown gives you just enough to see one more flop, play one more hand, or even turn the whole thing around," McEvoy adds.

## TIP 21: Hang On to a Lone Ranger

Six players remained in the annual $5,000 freeroll Texas hold'em tournament at my local card room. Pared down from a showing of over 40 entrants, six players were vying for the four payoff slots of $2,500, $1,500, $600 and $400. Button's suited A-K had just been drawn out on by a pocket pair of queens and he was a touch on tilt.

In the very next pot, when Player One raised in first position, Button called. The flop came A-10-4. Player One bet out and Button not only called, but threw in his last 11 chips, exclaiming, "See ya at the river!" That was the only place he saw, as Player One's pocket rockets left Button's weak 10-9 groveling in the dust of defeat.

Button made a short stack's most common mistake: Still steaming from his previous bad beat with big slick, he threw in his lone rangers (extra chips) and went all-in with a marginal hand. The two players to his left, who would need to take the next set of blinds, were both low on chips and close to elimination. Button could have stayed in the race for seven more hands with only his measly 11 chips, about 15 minutes of play, before having to post the mandatory blinds. Instead he hobbled himself by "tilting and tossing."

Players with short stacks late in a tournament often take unnecessary risks that eliminate them. Perhaps feeling their chances are too slim to survive, they lay across the railroad tracks waiting for the train to run over them. If you ever slide into this dementia, change your attitude. So long as you have a chip and a chair, you have a chance.

More tournament winners than you can count have been down to the green before making a comeback to win the roses. Tom Regan won the Bicycle Club's 1992 Oktober Pokerfest $300 lowball event for $13,680. He was down to two chips before he defeated his final opponents, one of whom was world champion Brad Daugherty. "If you're going to play lowball, it's better to be Regan than to be lucky," said L. P. Roach in *Card Player* magazine.

"The biggest tournament mistake a player can make is to give up, but sometimes players are in such pain, they throw in their chips just to bail out," opined Sykes. Winston Churchill put it this way: "Never ever ever ever ever give up!" I wonder if he played poker?

## The Ultimate Tournament Tip

No matter what ugly things happen to you in a tournament, keep a positive mental attitude. It doesn't matter if:

♠ Maniac draws out on you in a monster pot
♠ You fold the winning hand against Aggressor's bluff
♠ The dealer mistakenly mucks our winning pair of kings

♠ Slow Play sucks you into calling his raise on the river

♠ A misdeal is called when you're holding pocket aces

♠ You are dealt nothing but rags for the first two hours

You will always get drawn out on, fold a winner, fall victim to a slow play, get dealt a bag of rags, and sit at tables where dealers make mistakes. But this is the only chance you'll ever get to win *this* tournament.

Never fall victim to the one adversary who beats you more often than any other — yourself! Nothing will defeat you as quickly as losing focus and going on tilt. Be your own best ally, not your own worst enemy.

# CHAPTER 6

# 26 TOURNAMENT TRAPS

If every entrant played perfect tournament strategy and received his fair share of good cards, Lady Luck alone would award the crown — but they don't and she doesn't. Here is a list of errors that my grandfather would have titled either "Things I Wish I Hadn't Done" or "Things I Wish I Had Done." I don't know which is worse, but they all come under the heading of traps to avoid. They are a sort of ABC's of errors, a bowl of cold alphabet soup that you'd rather dump down the disposal than reheat.

## A. Playing Too Aggressively

Using maniac techniques to run over the game. Pushing a small edge even when it endangers your survival in the tournament. Never slowing down or changing gears during changing conditions. Betting a draw too strongly.

## B. Playing Too Timidly

Playing like a ring-game rock. Betting like a mouse when you should come out roaring like a lion. Not attempting to take out a short stack when you should.

## C. Making Too Many Rebuys

Exceeding your budget for the tournament, usually because you're playing too loose. Or because you won't accept stingy Lady Luck, who is keeping you in rags. Or because you thought that you needed that extra insurance you purchased with an unnecessary add-on in top chip position.

## D. Going All-In With a Bang

Throwing in those last few extra chips when losing them could eliminate you from the tournament instead of saving them for one more hand — the one that may be strong enough to send you to the final table rather than to the rail. Players often do this when they lose their concentration or when they go on tilt after a bad beat. In low-limit events, some players go all in on risky hands when their patience with the slow pace of the tournament grows thin and they decide that they would rather play in the faster side games than face the tournament's tedium. Translation: They get bored.

## E. Risky Confrontations in the Late Stages

Risking your good tournament standing by betting your marginal hand against someone of equal stack strength, with the possible result of reducing your chip mountain to a mole hill. Getting caught in a three-way struggle with another high stack and one contending low stack where you risk promoting the low stack's status if he wins the pot.

## F. Not Keeping Track of Your Chip Status

Making plays that are low percentage in relation to the size of your stack. Betting into an aggressive tall stack when you're in low or middle stack status.

Bucking another tall stack in the late stages when there are two or more other players in the pot and you are holding a mediocre hand.

## G. Not Playing Your Best Poker

Getting yourself into "pot lock" by entering a pot from early position in hold'em with a mediocre hand, or in seven-card stud with a rag pair and one of your rank on board, or in Omaha high-low with a hand such as J-9-3-2, and then calling a double-raise behind you. Or not playing the strength of the button against the blinds in hold'em or a boss front in seven-card stud against meek players to your advantage.

## H. Not Changing Gears When You Should

Remaining in fast gear when you should be shifting into low. Or vice-versa. Not adapting to changing table conditions by varying your style of play because you don't recognize that things have changed or because you don't have enough experience in tournament play to understand its importance or because you don't know how to do it.

## I. Letting Fear Dictate Your Actions

"You're comparing their outsides with your insides," is the way Sykes explained it. "You're all in a stew while they're looking cool." Sometimes you overprotect your big stack because you're afraid of losing; or when you have a short stack, you don't gamble enough because you're afraid of losing. Either way, you lose. Emotions make bad decisions.

## J. Over-Protecting the Lead

You shift into drift either from the fear of loss or from a lack of insight about how to play a big stack. Instead of playing solid poker, you nut up and start losing momentum. The smaller stacks begin stealthily moving up on you like masked bandits ready to rob you in the dark.

## K. Waiting Too Long for Premium Hands

In the very late stages, you overestimate the strength that you need to enter a pot, forgetting to change strategy when you're playing in a shorthanded game. Waiting for the nuts will drive you nuts (or out) at the final table.

## L. Misreading the Strength of Your Opponents

Not putting your opponent on the correct hand. You either judged it to be weaker than it was and you lost extra bets, or his hand was stronger than you thought and you lost extra bets. Either way, you lost.

## M. Not Putting a Short Stack All-In With Your Tall Stack

Perhaps you didn't count him down (count the number of chips he has left to bet), so you didn't know that one more bet would have put him all in. Maybe you forgot that the more competitors you can eliminate very late in the event, the better. Or was he your friend and you soft-played him?

## N. Soft-Playing a Friend

Not playing your hand for maximum value against an opponent because of your emotional feelings for him. Don't ever do this. It isn't fair to your other opponents, it isn't correct tournament strategy, and it reduces your chances of winning. Furthermore many people believe that soft-playing anybody in a tournament, including your mother, is unethical.

## O. Giving in to Pressure to Divide Top-Prize Money

A friend of mine arrived at the final table with a monster stack. She was competing in her first Las Vegas tournament and had outlasted eighty other players. She said no when the other players suggested a nine-way split, but gave in when they pressured her to divide it five ways. At the time that the deal was made, she had two-thirds of the chips on the table and wound up winning one-fifth of the prize money. Think before you split. Learn to negotiate at the final table.

## P. Pushing a Small Edge Too Aggressively in a multiway Pot

Going all the way to the river raising and reraising with just a fraction of an edge rather than waiting for better odds when you would have had the best of it. Staying in high gear when you should shift to low.

## Q. Going on Tilt

A loony has just drawn out on you. You're getting nothing but rags. The guy next to you is chain smoking into your nose mask. The dealer has just mucked your winners. You've become impatient with waiting for playable hands. You begin wondering why you play poker at all. Like a pinball machine, you begin bouncing around, splashing chips, losing.

## R. Becoming Distracted

A railbird is kibitzing with you. Your dentist just dialed your cell phone to cancel your appointment. The player on your left is a maniac and the one on your right is a talkaholic. Put on a pair of imaginary earmuffs and pretend you're deaf.

## S. Becoming Fatigued

You slept only four hours last night and the tourney has lasted two hours longer than you planned. Rest up or get up. Better yet, don't sit down in a tournament unless you've laid down long enough to feel your best.

## T. Playing Too Loose

Your discipline has gone out the door. You're feeling desperate to win a pot so you enter a lot of them with inferior cards. After all, you've seen plenty of other players win big pots with any two cards. Betting too many hands in the early stages is a common mistake in low-limit rebuy events. Don't waste your chips on rags or you'll end up wearing rags because you paid too much for the privilege of playing rags.

## U. Playing Too Tight

Rocks don't usually fare very well in tournaments. Although you occasionally will play rocklike poker, most of the time it's better to play tight-aggressive — and hope you've given just enough "loose" calls to convince your opponents that they should always call you. Or maintain a tight image and use it to run a bluff or pull off a steal.

## V. Not Sizing Up the Opposition

You've been watching the football game on the overhead television instead of your opponents, so you've missed detecting tells and betting patterns. If the only hand you play is your own, you aren't using one of the most important tournament tools of all: Playing people while playing poker.

## W. Playing Too Tight With a Short Stack

Although you have more to risk with a short stack (elimination, for example), you also have more to gain. Relatively speaking, your chips are worth more per chip than those of the big stacks. There comes a time when you just have to lay them all on the line by sending in your Davids and praying that they will slay the Goliaths.

## X. Playing Too Loose With a Tall Stack

Big stacks are not ATM cards. You cannot continually make small withdrawals and still hope to have enough left over to buy the family a big-screen TV. Eventually, your credit line gets maxed out.

## Y. Not Preparing Beforehand

Dashing from a rock concert to the tournament. Slamming the door on an angry spouse as you depart for the club. Leaving your bankroll on the dresser. Instead, take 30 minutes to prepare yourself strategically and psychologically.

# Z. Giving Up

Don't. Kenny Duggan won first place in the 1992 World Series of Poker pot-limit hold'em event against a record 134 entrants. "This was my first World Series event," he said, "and I was down to *two* chips — but within an hour, I had won the thing!" Plus $134,000 and a $5,000 gold bracelet.

# CHAPTER 7

# POKER POTPOURRI

Potpourri. A miscellany. A medley. In this chapter you'll find a collection of tournament concepts, strategies, quotes, commentary and major tournament profiles.

- ♠ Using In-Tell-I-Gence
- ♠ Putting Players On Hands
- ♠ The Art of the Poker Deal
- ♠ Tournament Etiquette
- ♠ A Date With Lady Luck
- ♠ The Laws Of Luck
- ♠ Tournaments In Action

## Common Types of Tells

What is the bettor doing right now as he bets? Is he fidgeting? (Probably a big hand.) Are his hands shaking? (He's either loaded with cards or with something just as potent.) Is he looking away from the flop? (Usually indicates a strong holding.) What did he do when the flop hit? Did his hand move toward his chips? (He's going to bet.) Did he continue to stare at it? (Probably a no-fit hand.) Did he look back at his cards? (With three flush cards on the flop, he likely has *one* of that suit.) Did he utter a disparaging remark? (He probably likes the flop.)

You can't possibly watch every opponent on every flop, so zero in on the key players at the table or the most dangerous opponents, such as the maniacs, because they're the ones you most want to defend against. Strong opponents, especially pros, usually have washed out most of their tells and are very difficult to read. Against them you try to find other clues, such as betting patterns and noticing the kinds of hands they show down on the end.

## Conversational Tells

"Can I raise?" Tight Ted asks and then does *not* raise — he wants a free card.

"Is it my bet?" Innocent Irene asks and then bets — she is loaded.

"I hate to make this call with these rags," declares Pessimist Paul — he's holding the nuts.

"Let's gamble!" Dandy Don exclaims throwing in his chips with reckless abandon. Nobody can beat him.

"I just love these tournaments and getting to play against all you tough guys, even if it did cost me a lot to enter and I'll have to work overtime next week," Chatty Cathy rambles as she fires in a bet — probably camouflaging a weak hand with an overlay of unrelated verbiage.

"*%#$@!" Silent Sam just made the absolute nuts.

"*%#$@!" Double-Deceptor Dan just missed his hand.

## Body Language

♠ Slouchy Sue suddenly sits erect — she is holding the boss hand.

♠ Pete Palsy's hands shake as he throws in his bet — a big, big hand.

♠ Sly Sam's looking away from the table while he makes his bet — his cards are so good that even he can't look at them without grinning.

♠ Fast Eddie flashes his cards to his next-door neighbor: probably a trash hand.

## Table Habits

♠ Neat stacks piled in pyramids: A controlled player (translation: a dangerous threat).

♠ Lucky charms: Believes the Poker Gods will protect him from weak play. (Just hope they don't.)

♠ Fast-betting out of character with his usually deliberate motions: Probably a weak holding, maybe a bluff.

♠ Hesitates and then reluctantly pushes out a wager: Watch out!

## Tournament Tells

A powerful tell that you can pick up in tournament action is how a player's chip position (stack size) seems to affect his style of play. For example, if an aggressive player with a short stack rushes to put in a raise, he may be bluffing in an attempt to build his stack — especially just before the increments increase or when he is next in line to take the big blind in hold'em. However if a usually passive player makes the same move, it is more likely that he has a strong hand.

Against a player whose movements are very fast, Sheahan suggested that you "make him sweat for a while by delaying your betting reaction. Even though you have no intention of calling, pause a while before mucking your hand. The mixture of fear and respect your delay might earn can work in your favor in a later confrontation."

Sometimes you may suspect that a player with a big stack is nursing his lead by playing too tight. Is he fearful of losing his top-dog position and is therefore playing too few hands? How can you take advantage of his apparent timidity or tight play? Consider playing more aggressively than you ordinarily would.

Watching the betting patterns of your tournament opponents also can give you a winning edge. Notice whether they usually bet a weak hand strongly — or often slow-play a big hand. A friend of mine who is a professional poker player also tries to determine their favorite betting round and adjusts his strategy to take advantage of their predictability. "If Joe has a big hand," he observed, "he'll usually wait till fourth street to bet it. So if I have a draw or maybe a middle pair, I'll usually take the free card he gives me on the flop or first street rather than value-bet it. That way, I save myself a bet if I miss." Caro's classic *Caro's Book of Poker Tells — The Body Language of Poker* is an expose of poker tells with photographs illustrating each of them.

## Putting Players on Hands

"How do I know what he has in the hole?" If pasteboards were transparent, it would make life easier but until that happens you may as well admit that unless a player turns his cards face up, you'll never know for sure. Accepting this uncertainty may help you in getting through agonizing postmortems over hands you didn't call — those times when you think that you might have had the best hand — when you self-flagellate by asking yourself "Why didn't I call?" even though not calling was probably a good decision.

And those times when you remember that, although it may be a mistake to make a call that loses you one bet, it is a far bigger error not to make a call that would have won the pot. A player I know calls when he's in doubt. "If I'm up against a loose player, a maniac or a loser, I'll call him, if for no other unscientific reason than to *know*. Morning-after nagging doubts don't bother me that way." Don't take this to mean that I am recommending this type of calling-station play in tournament action — but this guy probably gets a few more nights of good sleep than I do.

Putting players on hands is a skill requisite to winning at poker. Just as a detective uses inductive reasoning and clues to solve a perplexing case, good poker players use several techniques to figure out their opponents' most likely hands. Some of them include:

## Betting Patterns

Judging from the hands that you have seen an opponent show down at the end, and then recalling how he played them, ask yourself: With a weak hand, does he usually bet strongly from front position or does he usually check-call hoping for an inexpensive draw? Does he usually bet or raise with a strong holding? With the nut hand, does he ever slow-play? How often does he bluff? Does he usually wait until a later street to raise? What seems to be his favorite betting round?

Some players prefer betting or raising their strong hands on the turn rather than the flop. Others like to wait before they raise, especially when they are sitting in a late position, so ask yourself, "When does this guy usually give action?" The answer will help you decide your own betting strategy. For example, you may not wish to bet on the round *before* your opponent's usual betting street, thus saving yourself a bet or getting a free card in case you don't make your hand.

If you are a beginning or intermediate player, you may gain significant value from using a Player Profile notebook for the next few months in your local cardroom. Concentrate on one player at a time, answering each of these questions about him. You'll be surprised to find out how much you learn in a short while — and how much easier reading tells will become as you put more mileage under your poker belt.

## The Hands He Has Played

One of the best ways to put a player on a hand is to notice the cards that he has shown down at the end. Does he play nothing but high pairs and A-K suited in hold'em? Rolled-up trips, top pair, or three-flushes in stud? Only A-2-3-4 in Omaha high-low, or does he occasionally come in with middle suited connectors, two high pair double-suited, or hands such as 2-3-5-6?

Has he ever shown down rags in last position? Does he usually call in the small blind with marginal cards? In fact, does he ever call in the small blind? If he usually does *not*, then when he *does*, he probably has a strong hand.

If you usually play against the same opponents, charting is one way to determine their general starting requirements and playing patterns. Charting is similar to compiling player profiles. Make four columns on a pocket-sized note pad: Player, Position, Hand, and Action. Take notes for at least the first hour of your session. You'll probably discover that your key opponents employ a unique betting pattern, a personalized style of play. If you remember it the next time you play against them, you can use it against them. (All right, so everybody's asking to see what you're writing and they're goading you with "Are you writing a book? Am I in it?" Let it roll off your shoulders just as smoothly as when you begin raking in the tough guys' chips next time you confront them. And don't show anybody your notes.)

For example, you may discover that Big Al raises only with a pocket pair of aces or kings or A-K suited in the first two positions in hold'em and he never raises with A-K offsuit. He seldom plays anything except picture cards in any position. He plays very few hands and he usually bets in a straightforward manner, even with the nuts, rather than slow-playing. Now, here's a good guy to avoid being in a pot with if you have inferior cards, right? But what if you have suited connectors in the hole and no aces or faces appear on the flop? Knowing that he doesn't play those types of hands can give you an edge. It is possible that if you bluff-bet, he will fold.

In Omaha high-low, you discover from reviewing your chart and player profiles (as part of your pregame mental-conditioning) that Hal usually plays only low hands with an ace suited to a wheel card. Or in seven-card stud, you note that Sharon always slow-plays trips unless they're lower than nines, and she usually delays betting a high four-flush until fifth street, when she will almost always raise her strong draw against a weak board.

Using your charts and player profiles will give you the winner's edge in determining the strength of your opponents' hands and in predicting what they will do next. In tournaments where you know most of the players, this is invaluable information. When you do not know them, key in on a few players who seem to be the most dangerous rather than trying to get a handle on all of them.

## Degree of Looseness-Tightness

Does your opponent play marginal hands out of position? Is he a calling station? A maniac? A rock? Does he play stuff like J-6 suited in hold'em? Q-10-9-7 in Omaha high-low? Rag pairs in stud? Is he aggressive with a drawing hand or is he aggressive only when he has the nuts? How many hands does he play? A lot — he's loose; only a few — he's tight. How often does he raise, bluff and slow-play? "You should always be looking for general tendencies — who you think is playing a little bit conservatively, who's playing loose, who's playing solid, and who's gambling with a lot of marginal hands," McEvoy explains. "Pay close attention to what kinds of cards they call with, which hands they raise with, and the caliber of cards they turn over at the showdown."

## Current Status in the Game

What does he do when he's winning? Does he sit back on his lead and wait an hour for another starting hand? Or does he usually play the next hand after he wins a pot, possibly with inferior cards, or because he wants to play what he perceives as a rush? Does he play a rush aggressively? Does he bluff more when he's winning big, apparently taking advantage of his image? In other words, does he play tighter, looser or about the same as always when he is winning?

When he's losing, what does he do differently, if anything? Some players try to make up for losses by playing too many hands or by bluffing, often in an early or late position in hold'em or with a strong looking front in stud. Does he seem to take an inordinate number of flops when he's on a low stack? He may be on tilt, grasping at straws with rags. Or does he tighten up and play only premium hands until his luck changes? Is he grumbling about bad luck?

## Flop-Fitting Hands

Ask yourself, "Given this flop, what type of hand would a player bet with?" Here is an example: Aggressor raises from a front position in Texas hold'em and has two callers, Mid-stack and Button. The flop comes 2♦ 6♥ 7♥. Aggressor bets, Mid-stack calls and Button raises. If Aggressor raised before the flop with a high pair, he would bet his overpair on this flop. If Mid-stack usually plays high pairs, suited connectors, or suited paints from a middle position, he may have a flush draw. Button is likely to have an open-ended straight draw, two pair or maybe a low set.

If all this is true, Aggressor's best "out" may be hitting a card to his overpair to make trips. He might use this common business axiom in making his decision to call, fold or reraise Button's raise: "Knowing what I know now (conditions have changed), what is my best course of action?"

Another example: The flop comes K-J-3 offsuit. You are holding the J♠ 3♠ on the button and must decide whether to call the two bettors in front of you. What are the chances of their holding better cards than you do? A-K is considered to be a strong starting hand from any position, K-J is a common starting hand from middle position, and Q-10 or A-Q is also a middle starting hand. Therefore it is likely that you're up against either a king with a big kicker, a flush draw, a straight draw, an inside straight draw or a possible top two-pair. Your best out may be another trey — do you call, raise or fold?

The more experience you have and the more observant you become, the better your chances of accurately putting players on hands. But one thing is certain: If you are playing only one hand at the table — your own — you are at a distinct disadvantage in deciding your best strategy. Learn to recognize the clues your opponents leave at the "scene of the crime."

## A Word about Playing Low-Limit Freeze-out Events

In a freeze-out tournament you cannot rebuy when you go broke. What you see is what you get — when your starting stack of chips is gone, it's adios time. Because you cannot rebuy, surviving the early stage is of the utmost importance. Therefore you play only solid hands rather than ones that require a big draw to win. To put it another way, you must bring your A-game to the table with you and play very solid poker without being overly timid or unduly aggressive.

This advice may sound paradoxical if you have watched many World Series tournaments in which the leaders appear to play with undue aggression. However recall that they are competing in no-limit rather than limit play and the strategies are different. (Most of the high-limit players also know each other very well and can make highly accurate guesses as to the responses their opponents will make to their aggressive raises and other ploys.)

Caro suggests playing even more conservatively in no-rebuy tourneys than you would play in a ring game. The key is to play tight-aggressive. When you have a big hand, bet it strongly. Although you risk being an easy target for a steal if you play too tight, just remember that you cannot replenish your stack with a rebuy, so be reluctant to play marginal hands. When you don't hit the flop in hold'em or Omaha high-low, or improve your hand in seven-card stud, usually bow out early unless you have an unusually strong draw to the nuts. Playing selectively aggressive seems to be the ticket to success. Swoop down on them like an eagle when you've got it, but fly out the back door when you don't.

## The Art of the Poker Deal

The tournament payoff pie is often cut into pieces of different sizes than the chef ordered. The final two or three players (sometimes more) usually negotiate a deal among themselves to divide the total remaining prize money into equitable shares based on their relative chip status or negotiation prowess. Making a deal at the end happens about 90 percent of the time in low-limit tourneys.

Competitors base their decisions to terminate the tournament short of a final showdown on such factors as ending the stress and tedium of playing in survival mode, realizing the impact of luck at the final table, and the fatigue factor (some tourneys last into the early morning hours). After the deal has been made, one final hand sometimes is dealt to determine who gets the trophy, a practice that is typical of low-limit events but almost never is used in high-limit tournaments.

Ray Leitner listed other important reasons for making deals in his *Card Player* treatise on tournament money splits: "Are their opponents weak or strong? Who's in possession of the big stacks or has a little stack (weak or strong)? If it's a game of position, what position are they in?" If you are in the lead against a strong opponent(s), you may be more likely to want to deal than if your opponent is weak. If three of you are left and two of you have big stacks against one short stack, you probably will want to wait until the third stack bombs out. If you are trailing your opponents and are the next in line to take the big blind in hold'em, you are more likely to suggest a deal before you take the blind. However if you are on the button with the middle stack or the short stack, you may be less likely to deal.

Although you might think that the players in second or third position would suggest making the deal, deals usually are initiated by the chip leader. This is particularly true when the deal is being made between the final two players. The player in second place is guaranteed second-place money whereas the chip leader does not have a lock on first-place money. Therefore if a deal is discussed in a two-way split, it is the chip leader who usually brings up the subject.

In a three-way split of the final prize pool in the $200 Omaha high-low event of the 1993 Aladdin Oasis tournament, the final three were almost even in chips and voted for a split. "It frequently makes good sense to do business; because of the big luck factor, the lead can change every hand," the reporter wrote in *Card Player*. Max Stern was awarded first place and $8,760 based on his chip count, while Dennis Horton and Don Williams each received $8,000.

Leitner told the story of one of the best splits a player ever made. It seems that former world champion Bill Smith was in heads-up competition for first place against a vacationing lady player in a low-limit tournament at a locals' casino in Las Vegas. With 97 percent of the chips stacked in front of her, she suddenly asked him, "Do you want to split it? All I really want is the trophy." In his most controlled Texas drawl, Bill answered, "Hell, yeah. That'll be just fine with me, ma'am." As Leitner phrased it, "Not a bad deal for the good ole boy, huh?"

## Tournament Etiquette

This is a poker player's version of Emily Post, your guide to "prim and proper" poker manners at the tournament table. Most players take their tournaments seriously. They don't like loudmouths, greenhorns who don't know the tournament rules, and other types of people who either distract them or slow down the action (including dealers who are inept). Here is a brief rundown of tournament etiquette. Unfortunately, few such lists are ever posted in cardrooms. (Imagine my pleasure at finding a copy of this list tacked on the players' bulletin board at Crystal Park Casino in Compton, California, when I played a tournament there in 1999.)

☞ Don't show your hand to other players.

☞ Don't talk to railbirds.

☞ Don't throw cards.

☞ Don't announce another player's hand before he shows it down.

☞ Don't distract others.

☞ Don't talk to someone who is in a hand.

☞ Don't play table captain. That's the dealer's job.

☞ Don't make derogatory comments to either the dealer or your opponents.

☞ Do be a considerate smoker.

Of course, I know a player who likes to break these etiquette rules. He thinks it creates an obnoxious table image that gives him an edge over his opponents. Whether he's right about the edge is debatable, but I agree with him on one thing — he's definitely obnoxious.

Years ago I was playing against a field of 80 competitors in the first round of an Omaha high-low tournament at a Las Vegas casino. The dealer was faced with keeping the main pot plus five side pots correct. An argumentative player kept insisting that a mistake had been made on side pot two. Even after the dealer had called the tournament director to assist him in restoring order to the table, she continued her barrage of brickbats. Four minutes into this harangue, the dealer again called the director, proffered his resignation from employment with the casino, and headed for home lamenting, "I just can't take this anymore." The self-appointed table captainess remarked, "Well, he didn't have to get so huffy just because he made a mistake." Only one player rebutted her, commenting "Well, you *were* a little rough on him." (Incidentally, all the pots were correct.) One of the reasons why many players believe that the level of competence of tournament dealers is on the decline is because even competent dealers sometimes suffer abusive remarks and other behavior thrown their way by disconsolate (and rude) tournament players. Eventually, they leave the occupation for something less stressful.

I believe that the best way to conduct ourselves at the tournament table is to be civil and courteous to both our opponents and the dealers. Myself, I prefer relative silence at tournament tables — I'm not there to make new friends, just new money — but that doesn't mean that I'm unfriendly, just businesslike.

> *If you're not drained at the end of*
> *each day at the tournament,*
> *you're not giving your best effort.*
> *If you're not coming home mentally and*
> *physically worn out,*
> *you haven't played your best game.*
> —T.J. Cloutier

# Who Should Be Crowned World Champion of Poker?

The world championship of poker is determined by winning at a game that is rarely spread in casinos, no-limit Texas hold'em, which Brunson has described as "the Cadillac of poker." Why? Because that's the way Benny Binion designed it 33 years ago when he assembled the foremost poker players of that era (all of whom were road gamblers) to play the high-limit game with which they were most familiar, no-limit poker. But some poker experts believe that the crown should be awarded on a different basis.

Glenn Cozen, the '93 World Series runner-up, thinks dealer's choice would be a better format: "Not only must a player be strong in *all* games, but a new strategic element is added when one can pick a game he knows an opponent is weak at." David Sklansky said that a poker octathlon would be the fairest measure of a player's right to be crowned champion. "The games should include Texas hold'em, seven-card stud, stud eight-or-better, Omaha high, draw lowball, razz, draw high and Omaha high-low split. The game could be changed every 30 minutes. I think it's absurd that the world championship is in a game that is rarely played anywhere."

Perhaps a better title for such a competition would be the *World Poker Olympics*. Satellites could be staged all over the globe. Top players from poker's amateur and professional ranks probably would flock to the event, knowing that the contestant with the best all-around poker skills would have a shot at the crown, not just the one-in-a-million high roller who knows when to hold'em or fold'em in the elite society of no-limit hold'em. The Tournament of Champions, inaugurated in 1999 by co-founders Mike Sexton and Chuck Humphrey, took a step in that direction; however, the tournament was discontinued after 2001 because the founders were unable to attain their major goal, corporate sponsorship of the event.

# A Date With Lady Luck

Napoleon used an unusual selection practice in deciding whether a man would have "practical value" as a leader in his army. "Has he luck?" he always asked. Here is what some others have to say about the lady every gambler wants to court.

*Luck is like lightning — you can't bottle it
and you never know when or where it will strike.
So that leaves skill. And if you want to become a winner,
you'd better start developing some.*

**— Bobby Baldwin**

*Good luck and bad luck are synonyms, in most cases,
for good and bad judgment.*

**— A. Nony Mous**

*Luck favors the mind that is prepared.*

**— Louis Pasteur**

*Even at the final table, fast-action tournaments
can rapidly turn into a crapshoot.*

**— Tom McEvoy**

*The reason weaker players continue to play
against stronger competition is that there is luck involved.
Enough so that, even if a man finds himself outclassed,
he still might end up buying a new television
with a professional player's money.*

**— Doyle Brunson**

# Poker Tournament Tips from the Pros

*Most people are dogmatically convinced that luck*
*plays the most important role in winning and losing.*
*The prevalence of that flimsy theory is the greatest thing*
*that ever happened to gamblers.*

**— Tex Sheahan**

*Skillful players often moan because*
*there's too much luck involved in poker.*
*They feel it gives those "suckers" too much of a chance.*
*But those players wouldn't be there if it weren't for*
*this luck factor. Just why would they play*
*if they knew for sure they'd lose?*

**— Doyle Brunson**

*We can improve our luck by making ourselves*
*readier for the chances of life as they come to us.*
*Shakespeare wrote: "If it be not now,*
*yet it will come. The readiness is all."*

**— A. H. Z. Carr**

*Most people underrate luck in the short run*
*and overrate it in the long run.*
*In other words, a good player could have a losing week*
*but could never have a losing year.*

**— David Sklansky**

*Luck! There is such a thing*
*and I know that there is, because*
*it comes in two kinds. Good and bad.*

**— Nick "The Greek" Dandalos**

*His luck continued to run hot,*
*but his feet began to get cold.*

**— Bobby Baldwin**

*I don't trust on luck. I have to think fast and figure
my percentages. I can't relax for a second.
I tell you, gambling is hard work!*

— **Johnny Moss**

*Amateurs overemphasize luck
and pros overemphasize skill.
It takes both to win.*

**Tex Sheahan**

*The thoughtless, the ignorant and the indolent,
seeing only the effects of things and not the things
themselves, talk of luck, of fortune and chance.
Seeing a man grow rich, they say how lucky he is.
They do not see the trials and failures and struggles
he voluntarily encountered to gain his experience.*

— **James Allen**

*To be a winner, a man has to feel good about himself
and know he has some kind of advantage going in.
I never made bets on even chances.
Smart is better than lucky.*

— **Titanic Thompson**

*Anyone who does not know how
to make the most of his luck
has no right to complain if it passes him by.*

— **Cervantes**

*My luck went so bad that when I caught
the ace of spades, it had a
funeral parlor logo on it.*

— **Tex Sheahan**

*Luck is always gonna break even.*
*Everybody in the whole world is gonna get*
*the same amount of luck.*
— **Puggy Pearson**

*Luck cannot be shared,*
*and to try to do so means*
*risking its vanishing altogether.*
— **Jack Richardson**

*Lucky is winning in spite of all*
*the reasons why you shouldn't.*
—**L. P. Roach**

# The Laws of Luck

Coming from the old school, I was taught to hope for good luck but to count on hard work. "Nobody's gonna hand it to you on a silver platter," Grandpa used to say. So I learned the value of work early and picked up some academic training and job skills to ensure that my daily rations would always be on the table. But I have always been fascinated with luck — how you get it, why you lose it, why some people are luckier than others.

Soon after I began playing poker, I learned that skill alone is not enough. I also needed to exercise self-control, read people's hands and minds, keep track of the percentages, choose the best game, be patient, ad infinitum. And sometimes I needed to get lucky. Learned scholars, theoreticians, authors and journalists whose self-appointed mission is to teach us everything we've always wanted to know about poker sometimes minimize the role that luck plays in our fortune at the tables. But I believe that a compatible blend of skill *and* luck is required to become prosperous at playing poker.

Perhaps that's one reason why I like an audiocassette album I recently heard on my car stereo driving from the California desert (where I used to live) to the Nevada desert (where I *live*). Titled *The Universal Laws of Success and Achievement,* it was written and delivered by one of America's most respected business and motivational speakers, Brian Tracy. I met Tracy a few years ago in his mansion in Solana Beach, California, and became fascinated with his rags-to-riches story. In my automobile, however, I was more interested in the cassette titled "The Laws of Luck" than I was in his inspirational personal saga.

Tracy began by telling the story of a young entrepreneur who had been searching, against the advice of his peers, for a unique business idea from the East Coast that he could bring home to the West Coast. The day he stepped off the platform at his college graduation, he stepped onto the first plane headed for The Big Apple. During the four-hour flight, he struck up a conversation with the man sitting next to him, an entrepreneur who owned an East Coast franchise and had been looking in vain for a West Coast investor. Bingo! By the time they reached New York, the young man had bought an Orange Julius outlet that soon became a financial bonanza and led him to other winning investments. He was a millionaire by age 26.

Was this guy lucky or was he smart? To answer this question, Tracy details several forces that influence "getting lucky." Here are a few of the concepts he espouses.

## Law of Probability

The mathematical probability of an occurrence can be predicted with considerable accuracy from observation, measurement and experience. You can increase the probability of an event happening by increasing its number of occurrences. For example, Amoco has the best record of any oil company for finding new sources of petroleum. When asked why, the Amoco president replied, "We drill more holes."

Probability increases with persistence. Fortunately, people are always free to persist for as long as they choose and thus increase their chances for success. Unlike baseball, you are never out after only three strikes. "You are your own umpire in the ball game of life," says Tracy. Profound, huh?

How many tournaments did you enter before you won your first one? Or have you yet to win? How many more times to you plan to try? The great thing about tournaments is that you don't have to go to the dugout after three strikes — in fact you never have to retire unless you want to. The late Tex Sheahan won the Saddle West seven-card stud tournament at age 76. Johnny Moss won his third World Championship of Poker in 1974 when he was 68 years old. Doyle Brunson was 70 years old when he won his ninth World Series of Poker gold bracelet in 2003, more than any other player in history.

## Law of Attraction

What you are seeking is seeking you! You attract into your life the people and things most in harmony with your dominant thoughts. This is why expecting the best is so important to becoming lucky. Think only of being dealt what you want, *never* of what you don't want. Haven't you heard players remark, "I *knew* that lousy card would come on the river and ruin my hand!" Our thoughts often act like magnets, attracting their physical counterparts into our lives.

## Law of Clarity

"The clearer you are about what you want — and what you're willing to do to get it — the greater the probability that you will experience luck," says Tracy. When you clearly define your goals, you become more alert to opportunities that will lead you to attaining them, just as the young man on the airplane did.

## Law of Expectations

We don't always get what we *want* in life, but we usually get what we *expect* if we expect it long enough. You've heard of the self-fulfilling prophecy: A golfer who usually strokes a 75 hits a clean 32 on the front nine only to shoot a 45 on the back nine. Why? "I'm only a 75 golfer, not a 64," he says as he gets what he expects.

How often have you entered a tournament not expecting to win? Not expecting to be lucky? I believe this attitude often belies a basic lack of self-confidence. Winning requires competence *and* confidence, plus a positive self concept and positive expectations. Optimism, not pessimism.

I've heard poker players say, "I'd rather be lucky than good." It's somewhat like hearing a man say, "I'd rather be handsome than rich." What are these people trying to get at? Are they saying that you can't expect to be both? Why not? Me, I'd rather be lucky *and* good, handsome *and* rich.

If you understand and practice the laws of luck, *you* can become both successful and lucky at poker and at anything else you do in your life.

# Tournaments in Action
## 1992 World Series $1500
Limit Omaha Event

Two World Series of Poker champions, Tom McEvoy (1983) and Berry Johnston (1986), face off for two hours in heads-up action. When the chips settle, McEvoy takes first place for $79,200 with Johnston winning $39,600 for second. "With the exception of when I won the world championship, this was the most grueling tournament I've ever played. Actually, tonight's event was a better win because I was playing one of the best poker players in the world." It seems that the caliber of player they defeat is a source of pride for top tournament winners (in addition to the money and fame, of course).

## 1992 Winnin' O' the Green (Bicycle Club)

A record-smashing 860 players enter the $330 limit Texas hold'em event — 88 tables of tournament tension. At the final table, James Biby faces three opponents at the $3,000-$6,000 level. Entering a final hand with $86,500 in chips and A-K in the hole, he looks at a Q-10-7 flop. Biby calls two all-in bettors, who are holding Q-8 and 10-10, respectively. Against the odds, he makes a belly-buster straight on the river to knock them both out of contention, winning first place and $88,500.

Holding on for second spot and $55,000 is George Marlowe, who telephones me the next day to collect his "Winners Edge" certificate and to say some nice

things about *Poker Tournament Tips From The Pros.*
Marlowe goes on to take seventh place in the 1993
World Series $1,500 limit Texas hold'em event for
$13,800. Now that his name has appeared in this book,
George has undoubtedly become immortalized in the
annals of poker.

## 1993 World Series $1,500 Limit Hold'em

"I consider myself an amateur compared to Jack
Keller (1984 world champion). He's tough and I'm
stunned that I was able to beat him," comments Hugo
Mieth, retired chemical engineer and winner of the
$220,800 first-place money to Keller's second-place
$110,400. Third-place ($55,200) finisher Paul Conelly,
an antique toy dealer, was playing in only the second
tournament he had ever entered, proving once again
that tournament novices can play with the big boys.
Jack Keller goes on to win the $1,500 limit Omaha
event for $61,800, bringing his World Series winnings
to over $1,400,000 and proving once again that you can
bounce back from a loss. Of course, a $110,400 second-
place finish doesn't seem like too bad a "loss" to me.

## 1992 L. A. Classic (Commerce Casino)

Barbara Enright defeats four other world
champions in the ladies seven-card stud event for a
win of $7,400. Going to the final table with a big chip
lead, Enright keeps the pressure on her opponents
— which may not have been too hard to do since she
held quads twice. Guess Mike Caro was right when he
said, "Every tournament winner got lucky." Of course
Enright also is a very skillful player who won fifth
place in the $10,000 championship event at the World
Series of Poker in 1995 to become the only woman to

date who has made it to the televised final table in the no-limit hold'em finale.

## Three 3-Event Winners in Big Tournaments

Phil Helmuth, Jr., 1989 World Champion, wins three tournaments in the 1993 World Series: the $1,500 no-limit hold'em event, $2,500 no-limit hold'em event and the $5,000 limit hold'em tourney. He won a total of $472,400 for the three tournaments.     T e d Forrest, Best All-Around Player in the 1992 L. A. Poker Classic tournament, wins the $1,500 razz event, the $1,500 Omaha high-low split tourney and the $5,000 seven-card stud event at the 1993 World Series. Total winnings: $311,400.

Ken Buntjer wins three titles back-to-back at the 1993 Gold Coast Open: the one-rebuy limit hold'em event, the Omaha high-low event and the partners hold'em-Omaha high-low tourney. Total winnings: $52,000.

## Big Wins with Little Hands

Good, better, best — what does it take to win? "It doesn't take a big hand to win, it just takes the best hand," as McEvoy said. In the 1992 Oktober Pokerfest's hold'em shootout tournament, John Hiku calls Leon Begleries' all-in blind hand in heads-up play between the two finalists. With a board of 3-9-10-4-3, Hiku's J-4 wins with just a higher card than his opponent's 7-5. He took home $13,600.

In the final deal for the championship at the 1992 World Series of Poker, two small-time hands enter into heads-up battle for big-time money — Hamid Dastmalchi with 8-4, and Tom Jacobs holding J-7. With a flop of J-5-7, Jacobs is a strong favorite with two pair until the turn produces the six that Dastmalchi needs to make an inside straight. With no improvement on the river, Jacobs settles for second place to Hamid's $1,000,000 winning hand.

Holding a rag Q-7, Steve French calls Joe Macchiaverna who bets all-in with A-J in the final hand of the 1993 California State Poker Championship at the Commerce Casino. With a flop of 5-5-J followed by another five on fourth street, Macchiaverna's fives full of jacks looks indomitable — until a queen appears on the river and hands the $18,600 championship to French with fives full of queens.

## The 1993 World Series of Poker Final Table

The first time I ever watched the final table action at the World Series of Poker was in 1993 when I screeched into valet parking fresh off the freeway after making the five-hour drive from California. As I dashed for the grandstands, only three players remained at the final table in the waning moments of the Big One. Wedged between a sweaty 250-pounder and a smelly cigar smoker, I had a perfect view of the back of Glenn Cozen's head with both John Bonetti and Jim Bechtel in my peripheral vision. Somehow, I had thought that it would be more exciting, more glamorous. I guess seeing only chip mountains being shoved into the middle of the baize, rather than the cards that prompted their movement, seemed rather boring. But so what? I was there and I was part of the action.

I watched in awe as Bonetti went all-in with his A-K, pushing a Matterhorn stack into the center to match wits with Bechtel's pocket sixes. And I gasped as Bonetti lost it all, bowing to Bechtel's set of sixes that ousted his pair of kings on the K-6-4-J-Q board. A few hands later, I joined the crowd in applauding Bechtel as he ran Cozen out of the race with a lowly J-6 to win the final pot (and a million dollars) with a high-card, no-pair hand over Cozen's 7-4. Remembering a J-6 with which I once lost a $100 pot, I trailed out of the arena to enter a fray more suited to my abilities and bankroll, the $10-$20 hold'em game in Binion's cardroom.

## The 2000 World Series of Poker Final Table

The last time I watched the final-table play at the World Series was May, 2000, when I leisurely strolled into the tournament area a half hour before it began and was promptly escorted to a third-row seat in the VIP bleachers, thanks to T.J. Cloutier telling the guard that I was "a part of the family." The family to which T.J. was referring may have been the circle of poker authors of which I am a member, or the corps of *Card Player* columnists to which both T.J. and I belong.

T.J. had some juice with the guard, of course, because he was among the six finalists at the final table, albeit low man on the totem pole with only $216,000 in chips against chip-leader Chris Ferguson's $2,853,000. Combined with his uncanny ability to read his opponents, his wizardry at no-limit hold'em, and his indomitable table presence, all Cloutier needed now was some juice with Lady Luck.

I watched with shock as players went all-in in rat-a-tat machine gun action, an anomaly at the final table of the Big One where players usually grind it out tediously trying to move up the enormously profitable ladder. Not this time. On only the second hand, Roman Abinsay bit the dust with A-Q against Ferguson's pocket eights. A short time later, Jim McManus joined him in the spectators' bleachers when he pitted his

A-2 against Steve Kaufman's A-Q. "Wow, in only 30 minutes or so, T.J. already has won an additional $443,360," I thought, "and he hasn't even played a hand yet!" I was impressed.

Not long afterward, T.J. moved up another $78,240 on the pay scale by watching Hasan Habib's K-Q get drowned in the undertow of Ferguson's A-K, increasing the top dog's already massive chip lead. All T.J. had to do now to become the all-time leading money winner at the World Series was outlast Steve Kaufman. Ferguson turned promise into reality when he made trip tens to knock Kaufman out in third place.

Unlike the play at the 1992 final table, this action was far from a yawner. These guys had come to play poker, to gamble, to entertain us. This was High Noon, the shoot-out at the OK Corral, and I was a part of it. I was hyped.

As Ferguson and Cloutier assembled for the final heads-up duel to crown the king of poker, I reflected upon the interviews that I had written for each of them in *Card Player* magazine. Ferguson, the quiet, long-haired, erudite scholar with the Ph.D. in computer science, a man highly respected in the poker world as a supreme tactician − and all-around good guy. Cloutier, the hefty former professional football player and Army veteran, the master story teller whose tales about his years as a road gambler have entertained players at poker tables across the globe, a man highly respected in the poker world as probably the best no-limit hold'em tournament player ever − and all-around good guy.

A huge chip dog to Ferguson, Cloutier began chipping away at the leader of the pack until he finally drew even with him. "How can anyone come from that far back?" I thought. Yet Cloutier had made the journey in record time, a smooth trip over the bumpy roads of tournament poker. After about two hours of dueling in the heat of what seemed like a thousand camera strobes, it happened. The hand. The showdown.

As Ferguson and Cloutier moved all their chips into the middle of the table, the audience fell mute except for the gasps of awe at seeing close to $2.5 million in chip castles towering between the soon-to-be crowned champion and runner-up. I was breathless when Cloutier turned over his A-Q, amazed that Ferguson had only an A-9 to fight the battle for the bracelet and the bucks. The flop floated onto the table: 2-K-4. Then the turn card bounced out: another king. Finally the river card rolled itself over: a nine, a lowly nine, but just enough to elevate Ferguson to the height of his poker career.

What a trip this 2000 final table had been! Two world-class players, both winners, both gentlemen. But only one had enough juice with Lady Luck to win it all.

## CHAPTER 8

# A TOURNAMENT TALE

◆

## The Farmer, The Cowboy and Lady Luck

Farmer ambled into the only cardroom in town ten minutes before the tournament began, his thinning gray hair still damp from the shower that had recently rinsed the smell of hay from his sun-dried arms and face.

"Hey, Farmer, you here to snap up some greens?" Old Elmer greeted him from the corner table where he held daily council from inside a permanent halo of Camel smoke that spiraled from the cigarette glued between his fingers.

"Gonna see what I can do to you boys this time," Farmer replied, heading for the freshly brewed coffee sitting on the side table beneath a movie poster advertising *A Big Hand For The Little Lady.* "All you need is a little luck" it read.

In the far corner stood three of the tradesmen-poker players who had helped refurbish the Garden Club when it expanded, adding one mega-sized new hold'em table that nobody liked because of its "unfriendly" dimensions. Consequently dealers wrapped their Christmas presents on it and "nooners" used it as a dining table.

Billy-D, a club regular who built the mahogany cage, kibitzed with Joey, who installed the maroon and yellow carpet, and Red, who had painted the walls a mellow yellow. They were laying odds on who would win the annual $5,000 freeroll Texas hold'em event sponsored by Lucky Louie, the Garden Club owner, as a gesture of his appreciation for the regulars who fed his hungry drop boxes their daily bread.

"If J.D. catches some cards, he'll run over the table like a Mercedes with no brakes," Joey speculated. Red countered, "He'll have a helluva time bumping Cowboy out of it, as lucky as he's been running."

"Don't count Keno out. He might be a rock but he's aggressive when he's hitting," added Joey. Under the subterfuge, each man was assigning a toughness index to his competitors, building up his own confidence to try to outrun everybody else and win the $2,500 first-place money and the big, flashy trophy that went with it.

Oblivious to the chatter, J.D. was sizing up the field. He knew them well, their betting habits, their level of expertise, even their warts. "It ain't gonna be easy," he mused. Although he'd won several Las Vegas tournaments, J.D. felt that some of the players in his hometown game were as tough as the competition in Glitter Gulch. In fact, a few of them were pros who made a decent living from traveling between the Garden Club, Las Vegas and the Southern California card rooms.

Cowboy was adjusting his sweat-stained Stetson and putting his usual friendly make on Liz, the cardroom queen, who often ran over the Omaha high-low game but was a loser at hold'em. She was repeating her tournament strategy to herself while feigning attention to both Cowboy and Keno, an alligator with floppy jowls and paunchy belt line who disguised himself as an amiable lap dog.

Crouching just beneath this smoke screen of small talk, ready to pounce at the drop of a card, lay a tiger of tension peculiar to all poker tournaments. Tension spawned of the lure of easy money, expectation, competition, pride and fear.

Twenty-seven of Oak Valley's finest cardsmiths gravitated to the three cleanly brushed hold'em tables as Louie spread the cards to draw for seats and Texas Tiny set the time clock to begin the holiday tournament. Perusing the lineup at table three, Liz moaned, "Why do I *always* draw a table with all the sharks?" which was her way of patronizing her male cohorts. She was right: an easy lineup it was not.

There was Joey, whom she both respected and feared; Old Elmer, the aging and faded lowball champion; Keno, the alligator-accountant who squeezed in some office hours between poker sessions; and J.D., who owned a monopoly on the local mini-storage business.

And there was Red, the steamer who could burn up more chips than a forest fire; Farmer, rumored to be the wealthiest man in the county; Billy-D, the slowplay artist; and the inscrutable Cowboy, a poker pro whose facial expressions disappeared during a hand.

Inching its way like a snail through two hours of tight play and escalating blinds, the tournament ground down to the final table. The Garden City regulars had gone through sporadic sparring for position, fast-action flurries and last-ditch desperation calls. Of the nine survivors, three committed major tournament errors at the money table. Look for them as some of the final action is recounted here.

In first position with pocket sevens, Old Elmer enters the pot with a raise. On a short stack, Joey calls with pocket eights in the third seat. Billy-D calls all-in with 5♦ 7♠ in the Big Blind. The flop comes 4♦ 5♥ 10♠.

Old Elmer bets with his middle pocket pair and Joey calls with his eights. The turn adds the 7♦, giving Elmer a set. Drawing to an inside straight, Joey calls Old Elmer's bet, leaving him with only one chip in his stack. The river card shows the 8♦. Joey's trip eights on the river wins the pot.

Who made the error? Holding a middle-pair and a big stack, Old Elmer's entering raise with pocket sevens was correct for final-table play. With his tight image, he may not get any callers and win the pot outright. With the big blind coming up in two hands, Joey correctly calls with a pocket pair and a short stack. On the flop, he holds what he believes is probably the second-best pair and calls.

With his lucky set of sevens on the turn, Elmer bets out again. At this point, Joey reasons that he still has second-best pair with a belly-buster straight draw — and only enough money left for the big blind. "I had no shot at a tournament win if I didn't win that hand. I had to call to have any chance at all because the winner of that pot would likely become the tournament leader."

All-in before the flop with his 7-5 offsuit, Billy-D's confidence at flopping middle pair rose even higher when he made two pair on the turn. But the river proved even more fatal to him than to Old Elmer. "I called the raise in the small blind, putting both Old Elmer and Joey on high pairs and hoping that with the big cards out, I'd have a chance with middle-connectors. Besides, I didn't have enough chips left to be competitive and decided to take a stand right then."

But he later admitted that maybe he made a mistake. "If I had it to do all over again, I would have considered the fact that on the next deal, I'd have the button and could wait for seven hands to be dealt some stronger starting cards. Guess I should've waited!"

A pair of pocket eights also decided another pivotal hand in the tournament. Three players had limped in when J.D., sitting on the button, peeked at his cards, 8-7 offsuit. With a tall stack, strong table image, and good position, he called the multiway pot with his rag connectors. Holding pocket eights and sitting in the small blind, Liz raised. The three limpers folded, leaving the dirty work to J.D. Seeing that Liz had only one-half a bet remaining in her stack, J.D. reraised her all-in. The flop came Q-4-5, followed by a three on the turn and a six on the river. When J.D. turned over his 8-7 for a straight, Liz joined the railbirds at the snacks table.

With four players who could reraise her, Liz was overly-aggressive with a middle pocket pair, a short stack, *and* a weak table image. Advance planning would have told her that if anyone chose to reraise, she would either have to call all-in or fold with only one-half a bet remaining in her puny stack. If she had just called to see the flop, and then mucked her hand when she didn't hit it, Liz would have had the button on the very next deal, along with seven extra chances to stay in action. J.D.'s reraise on the button demonstrates the power of a big stack and superior position in tournament play.

Six players remained in the tournament with a four-spot payoff. Farmer's pocket queens had just knocked Red out of third chip position when he caught a third "mop squeezer" on the river and beat Red's suited A-

K. On the very next hand, sitting on the button with a suited 10-7 *and* still fuming from his bad beat, Red called Cowboy's front-position raise. The flop came with A-10-4 rainbow. In answer to Cowboy's bet from the front, Red threw in his last few chips, saying, "See ya at the river!" When Cowboy exposed his pocket rockets, Red shot from the room like a rocket. Prudence, however, prevailed over rage as Red soon returned to join his other cronies and Liz for the free snacks Louie had ordered from the next-door Chinese takeout kitchen.

If Red had been monitoring his opponents' stacks, he would have noticed that Joey held an even lower stack than he did. Since Joey would have to take the big blind on the next deal (putting him all in), Red should not have called the preflop raise. But he was still angry about his previous bad beat. "What's the use when I can't even win with Big Slick?" he moaned. And so, giving up hope, he also gave up what could have been at least a $500 payday. Emotions make bad tournament decisions.

Three tournament mistakes, three money dropouts. Keno survived, however, by making a class laydown that helped him finish in the money. In first position with a pair of aces, J.D. raised the pot coming in. Keno reraised in fifth position with kings in the hole and just called J.D.'s final reraise. With a nothing flop, J.D. bet his pocket rockets and Keno folded his two cowboys. "I had to respect his bet from an early seat. I know how he plays so I knew he wasn't bluffing. Since I had the power of position over him, J.D. had to be holding pocket aces to bet into me."

Such is the drama of a low-stakes poker tournament, the kind most of us play everyday in our hometown cardrooms or in Las Vegas. Not the million-dollar payoff tourneys with their star-studded lineups. Not the no-limit marathons where intimidating world-class players nonchalantly push mountains of chips into the middle. No, just the bread-and-butter matching of wits between low-stakes cardroom regulars with high-stakes casino ambitions.

Oh yes, about the final outcome. Cowboy placed second with Keno taking third and Joey hanging on for fourth. Of course, the dark-horse Farmer won the whole enchilada when his 9-7 offsuit rounded up a gutshot straight on the river and gunned down Cowboy, who rode off into the tournament sunset cursing the bad beat he had taken with his pair of jacks.

"What're you fixin' to do with all that prize money of yours?" Liz inquired of the victorious Farmer.

"Bail it, darlin', just like I do my hay!" he proudly announced. Which is another reason why Farmer is still one of the wealthiest men in the county.

# Tournament Terminology

**Add on.** A stack of chips that players have the option to buy at the end of the rebuy period in a tournament. The last opportunity you have to buy chips in a rebuy event.

**Backer.** Someone who pays the entry fees for a tournament player with whom he will split the rewards at the end of the event.

**Buy-in.** The amount of money that you pay to enter a tournament, for which all players receive a fixed number of chips.

**Case chips.** Your last chips.

**Change gears.** Change your style of play from aggressive to passive, from tight to loose, from fast to slow to adjust to changing table conditions.

**Chip status.** How the number of chips that you have in front of you compares to those of your opponents.

**Confrontation.** A big pot that usually is contested heads-up and often significantly changes the chip status of the opponents or alters the outcome of the tournament.

**Get full value.** Betting, raising and reraising in order to manipulate the size of the pot so that you will be getting maximum pot odds if you win the hand.

**Increment.** The increase in chips that it takes to post the blinds or antes at the start of a new round in a tournament. For example, if the blinds rise from $10-$20 to $20-$40, the increment has doubled.

**Limp in.** Enter the pot by calling rather than raising another player's bet. A limper is a player who has entered the pot by just calling the opening bet.

**Make a deal.** Negotiate a new way of dividing the chips among the top finishers at the last table in a tournament.

**Make a move.** Try to bluff.

**Maniac.** A very aggressive player who often plays hands that solid or conservative players would not consider.

**Nuts.** The best possible hand.

**Out.** A card that will make your hand.

**Payout.** The prize money you win at the end of the event.

**Play back.** Respond to an opponent's bet by raising or reraising.

**Play fast.** Aggressively bet a drawing hand to get full value for it if you make it.

**Rag.** A board card that doesn't help you.

**Read.** Determining what your opponent is holding or the significance of his betting strategy.

**Rebuy.** The amount of money that you pay to add a fixed number of chips to your stack in a tournament.

Rebuy period. The time frame within which you are allowed to make a rebuy in a tournament (usually the first three rounds).

**Ring game.** Not a tournament game. A cash game that you play while you are not in tournament action.

**Rock.** A very conservative player who always waits for premium cards before he plays a hand.

**Round.** The predetermined length of time that each betting increment is in force during a tournament (20 minutes, one hour, and so on).

**Run over.** Playing aggressively in an attempt to control your opponents.

**Solid player.** An accomplished player who employs optimal strategy at all times.

**Survival.** Playing conservatively rather than betting for maximum value in an attempt to last longer in the tournament.

**Tell.** A playing habit that a player consistently uses at the table which enables his opponents to tell what he is holding or what he is likely to do during the play of a hand.

**Where you're at.** You know the value of your hand compared to your opponent's hand.

# Bibliography of Sources Quoted

Bobby Baldwin, *Tales Out of Tulsa*. An educational and entertaining book by the 1978 world champion of poker.

Jon Bradshaw, *Fast Company*. This compelling collection of stories about the fascinating careers of legendary gaming figures Pug Pearson, Bobby Riggs, Minnesota Fats, Tim Holland, Johnny Moss and Titanic Thompson hooked me into reading it nonstop.

Doyle Brunson, *According to Doyle*. Brunson at his best. The subtitle says it all: "Poker Wisdom from the World Champion." Brunson's "other" book is *Super/System*.

Mike Caro, *Caro's Fundamental Secrets of Poker*. The "mad genius" hits the bull's-eye once again with this easy-to-read compendium of gaming advice. *The Body Language of Poker* (formerly titled *Mike Caro's Book of Tells*) has become the classic in its field. In fact Caro himself is a classic.

A.H.Z. Carr, *How to Attract Good Luck*. The quaint 1950s language of Carr's book adds color to its provocative title.

Bob Ciaffone, *Omaha Hold'em Poker*. Nicknamed "The Coach" by professional poker players, Ciaffone took third place at the 1987 World Series of Poker. This intelligent book includes discussions of high Omaha, Omaha high-low, and tournament play.

T.J. Cloutier, *Championship No-Limit & Pot-Limit Hold'em*. The player who has won more money at tournament poker than any other player in history delivers the goods in this clearly-written book on how to play the poker game that took him to the top of his profession. Written with Tom McEvoy, with whom Cloutier also co-authored *Championship Hold'em*, *Championship Omaha*, and *Championship Tournament Practice Hands*.

Tom McEvoy, *Tournament Poker*. This book is considered by most pros to be the "bible of tournament poker." The 1983 World Champion of Poker, McEvoy details his winning formula and outlines strategies for all the poker games played at the World Series.

# Sources

Mason Malmuth, *Gambling Theory and Other Topics*. Trained as a statistician, Malmuth is well known as a columnist and authority on probability. The sections on tournament play are helpful.

Tex Sheahan, *Secrets of Winning Poker*. The "dean of poker columnists" reprises 15 years worth of his best columns.

Shane Smith, *Omaha High-Low Poker*. This easily read and highly informative text is targeted for novice and intermediate players and includes a chapter on Omaha high-low tournament strategy. Smith also penned *Low-Limit Casino Poker*, a useful guide designed especially for novices on how to win at four casino poker games.

Bill "Bulldog" Sykes, *Poker! Las Vegas Style*. Blending wisdom and wit, Sykes' reprise of his *Card Player* columns is filled with winning advice, colorful anecdotes and homespun humor.

Articles quoted from *Card Player* magazine include: Michael Cappelletti, "General Tournament Strategy" and "Tournament Strategy at the Final Table," 11/15/91 and 11/29/91. Bob Ciaffone, coverage of the 1991 World Series of Poker, 6/14/91. W. Lawrence Hill, "The 1992 World Champion," 6/12/92. Ray Leitner, "Just When You Think You've Heard Everything," 4/20/90. Mason Malmuth, "Two Tournament Mistakes," 6/14/91. L.P. Roach, "Oktober Pokerfest: A Fall Hit," 10/30/93. "World Series of Poker Sets Record," 6/4/93. Max Shapiro, "Crazy Man Wants World Title," 7/30/93. Mike Caro, "Profitable Poker Insights," 8/4/2000. Tom McEvoy, "Right Play, Wrong Result," 10/13/2000.

Interviews in the early 1990s with Bill "Bulldog" Sykes, Tex Sheahan and Ron Limuti in Las Vegas; and Norm Michaud and Richard White in Bakersfield, California. Conversations in the early 2000s with T.J. Cloutier, Tom McEvoy, Byron "Cowboy" Wolford, Bill Boston and Don Vines in Las Vegas, Reno and Los Angeles.

# Poker Tournament Tips from the Pros

*It is ten times worse to commit a mistake in a tournament
as it is to make that same mistake in a cash game
where you can go to your pocket for more money.*
— **T.J. Cloutier**

*Getting married to a hand is one of the biggest mistakes
that a tournament players can commit.
Making proper laydowns is essential to your success.*
— **Tom McEvoy**

*In regular play, skill and a bankroll can compensate
for a few early lapses or errors, but in tournaments,
when you are tapped, you're out. And you
can't afford many mistakes when you are
skating on thin ice.*
— **Tex Sheahan**

*Nobody has ever won a tournament
in the first three hours of play.*
— **T.J. Cloutier**

*You have to play a patient, controlled game,
steadily increasing your stack with good, solid play.
And you must maintain strict control of your emotions.*
— **Tom McEvoy**

*How much does luck have to do with winning
tournaments? I think the most reasonable mathematical
definition would result in an estimate of
75 percent luck and 25 percent skill.*
— **Chris Ferguson**

## Poker Tournament Tips from the Pros

*Even highly skilled players should expect*
*to lose tournaments unless their luck is*
*much better than average that day.*
— **Mike Caro**

*Tournament winners combine extremely good judgment*
*with some lucky breaks. The trick is to survive long enough*
*to put yourself in the position to get lucky.*
— **Tom McEvoy**

*If you take poker seriously,*
*then you ought to treat it like a business.*
*But who says you have to take it seriously?*
*Poker is great recreation.*
— **Doyle Brunson**

*I don't have much regard for money.*
*Money's just paper to gamble with, and when*
*I leave the table, I don't give it no nevermind.*
*But Virgie, my wife, well, Virgie's a millionaire.*
— **Johnny Moss**

*There are no maniacs in a $10,000 tournament.*
— **Bill "Bulldog" Sykes**

*Every conscious act requires risk.*
*Every conscious act requires decision.*
*Put these two facts together and you realize that*
*the secret to life is not to avoid gambling,*
*but to gamble well.*
— **Mike Caro**

# GREAT POKER BOOKS
## ADD THESE TO YOUR LIBRARY - ORDER NOW!

**TOURNAMENT POKER** by Tom McEvoy - Rated by pros as best book on tournaments ever written, and enthusiastically endorsed by more than 5 world champions, this is a must for every player's library. Packed solid with winning strategies for all 11 games in the World Series of Poker, with extensive discussions of 7-card stud, limit hold'em, pot and no-limit hold'em, Omaha high-low, re-buy, half-half tournaments, satellites, strategies for each stage of tournaments. Big player profiles. 344 pages, paperback, $39.95.

**OMAHA HI-LO POKER** by Shane Smith - Learn essential winning strategies for beating Omaha high-low; the best starting hands, how to play the flop, turn, and river, how to read the board for both high and low, dangerous draws, and how to win low-limit tournaments. Smith shows the differences between Omaha high-low and hold'em strategies. Includes odds charts, glossary, low-limit tips, strategic ideas. 84 pages, 8 x 11, spiral bound, $17.95.

**7-CARD STUD (THE COMPLETE COURSE IN WINNING AT MEDIUM & LOWER LIMITS)** by Roy West - Learn the latest strategies for winning at $1-$4 spread-limit up to $10-$20 fixed-limit games. Covers starting hands, 3rd-7th street strategy for playing most hands, overcards, selective aggressiveness, reading hands, secrets of the pros, psychology, more - in a 42 "lesson" informal format. Includes bonus chapter on 7-stud tournament strategy by World Champion Tom McEvoy. 160 pages, paperback, $24.95.

**POKER TOURNAMENT TIPS FROM THE PROS** by Shane Smith - Essential advice from poker theorists, authors, and tournament winners on the best strategies for winning the big prizes at low-limit re-buy tournaments. Learn the best strategies for each of the four stages of play—opening, middle, late and final—how to avoid 26 potential traps, advice on re-buys, aggressive play, clock-watching, inside moves, top 20 tips for winning tournaments, more. Advice from McEvoy, Caro, Malmuth, Ciaffone, others. 144 pages, paperback, $19.95.

**WINNING LOW LIMIT HOLD'EM** by Lee Jones - This essential book on playing 1-4, 3-6, and 1-4-8-8 low limit hold'em is packed with insights on winning: pre-flop positional play; playing the flop in all positions with a pair, two pair, trips, overcards, draws, made and nothing hands; turn and river play; how to read the board; avoiding trash hands; using the check-raise; bluffing, stereotypes, much more. Includes quizzes with answers. Terrific book. 176 pages, 5 1/2 x 8 1/2, paperback, $19.95.

**WINNING POKER FOR THE SERIOUS PLAYER** by Edwin Silberstang - New edition! More than 100 actual examples provide tons of advice on beating 7 Card Stud, Texas Hold 'Em, Draw Poker, Loball, High-Low and more than 10 other variations. Silberstang analyzes the essentials of being a great player; reading tells, analyzing tables, playing position, mastering the art of deception, creating fear at the table. Also, psychological tactics, when to play aggressive or slow play, or fold, expert plays, more. Colorful glossary included. 288 pages, 6 x 9, perfect bound, $16.95.

**WINNER'S GUIDE TO TEXAS HOLD 'EM POKER** by Ken Warren - This comprehensive book on beating hold 'em shows serious players how to play every hand from every position with every type of flop. Learn the 14 categories of starting hands, the 10 most common hold 'em tells, how to evaluate a game for profit, and more! Over 50,000 copies in print. 256 pages, 5 1/2 x 8 1/2, paperback, $14.95.

**KEN WARREN TEACHES TEXAS HOLD 'EM** by Ken Warren - In 33 comprehensive yet easy-to-read chapters, you'll learn absolutely everything about the great game of Texas hold 'em poker. You'll learn to play from every position, at every stage of a hand. You'll master a simple but thorough system for keeping records and understanding odds. And you'll gain expert advice on raising, stealing blinds, avoiding tells, playing for jackpots, bluffing, tournament play, and much more. 416 pages, 6 x 9, $24.95.

# THE CHAMPIONSHIP BOOKS
## POWERFUL BOOKS YOU MUST HAVE

**CHAMPIONSHIP OMAHA (Omaha High-Low, Pot-limit Omaha, Limit High Omaha)** by T. J. Cloutier & Tom McEvoy. Clearly-written strategies and powerful advice from Cloutier and McEvoy who have won four World Series of Poker titles in Omaha tournaments. Powerful advice shows you how to win at low-limit and high-stakes games, how to play against loose and tight opponents, and the differing strategies for rebuy and freezeout tournaments. Learn the best starting hands, when slowplaying a big hand is dangerous, what danglers are and why winners don't play them, why pot-limit Omaha is the only poker game where you sometimes fold the nuts on the flop and are correct in doing so and overall, how can you win a lot of money at Omaha! 230 pages, photos, illustrations, $39.95.

**CHAMPIONSHIP STUD (Seven-Card Stud, Stud 8/or Better and Razz)** by Dr. Max Stern, Linda Johnson, and Tom McEvoy. The authors, who have earned millions of dollars in major tournaments and cash games, eight World Series of Poker bracelets and hundreds of other titles in competition against the best players in the world show you the winning strategies for medium-limit side games as well as poker tournaments and a general tournament strategy that is applicable to any form of poker. Includes give-and-take conversations between the authors to give you more than one point of view on how to play poker. 200 pages, hand pictorials, photos. $29.95.

**CHAMPIONSHIP HOLD'EM** by T. J. Cloutier & Tom McEvoy. Hard-hitting hold'em the way it's played today in both limit cash games and tournaments. Get killer advice on how to win more money in rammin'-jammin' games, kill-pot, jackpot, shorthanded, and other types of cash games. You'll learn the thinking process before the flop, on the flop, on the turn, and at the river with specific suggestions for what to do when good or bad things happen plus 20 illustrated hands with play-by-play analyses. Specific advice for rocks in tight games, weaklings in loose games, experts in solid games, how hand values change in jackpot games, when you should fold, check, raise, reraise, check-raise, slowplay, bluff, and tournament strategies for small buy-in, big buy-in, rebuy, incremental add-on, satellite and big-field major tournaments. Wow! Easy-to-read and conversational, if you want to become a lifelong winner at limit hold'em, you need this book! 320 Pages, Illustrated, Photos. $39.95

**CHAMPIONSHIP NO-LIMIT & POT LIMIT HOLD'EM** by T. J. Cloutier & Tom McEvoy The definitive guide to winning at two of the world's most exciting poker games! Written by eight time World Champion players T. J. Cloutier (1998 Player of the Year) and Tom McEvoy (the foremost author on tournament strategy) who have won millions of dollars playing no-limit and pot-limit hold'em in cash games and major tournaments around the world. You'll get all the answers here - no holds barred - to your most important questions: How do you get inside your opponents' heads and learn how to beat them at their own game? How can you tell how much to bet, raise, and reraise in no-limit hold'em? When can you bluff? How do you set up your opponents in pot-limit hold'em so that you can win a monster pot? What are the best strategies for winning no-limit and pot-limit tournaments, satellites, and supersatellites? You get rock-solid and inspired advice from two of the most recognizable figures in poker — advice that you can bank on. If you want to become a winning player, a champion, you must have this book. 209 pages, paperback, illustrations, photos. $39.95

**Order Toll-Free 1-800-577-WINS or use order form on page 144**

# POWERFUL POKER SIMULATIONS
## A MUST FOR SERIOUS PLAYERS WITH A COMPUTER!
### IBM compatibles CD ROM Windows 3.1, 95, and 98 - Full Color Graphics

**Play interactive poker** against these **incredible** full color poker simulation programs - they're the absolute **best** method to improve game. Computer players act like real players. All games let you set the limits and rake, have fully programmable players, adjustable lineup, stat tracking, and Hand Analyzer for starting hands. Mike Caro, the world's foremost poker theoretician says, "Amazing...A steal for under $500." Includes free telephone support. **New Feature!** - "Smart advisor" gives expert advice for every play in every game!

**1. TURBO TEXAS HOLD'EM FOR WINDOWS - $89.95** - Choose which players, how many, 2-10, you want to play, create loose/tight game, control check-raising, bluffing, position, sensitivity to pot odds, more! Also, instant replay, pop-up odds, Professional Advisor, keeps track of play statistics. Free bonus: Hold'em Hand Analyzer analyzes all 169 pocket hands in detail, their win rates under any conditions you set. Caro says this "hold'em software is the most powerful ever created." Great product!

**2. TURBO SEVEN-CARD STUD FOR WINDOWS - $89.95** - Create any conditions of play; choose number of players (2-8), bet amounts, fixed or spread limit, bring-in method, tight/loose conditions, position, reaction to board, number of dead cards, stack deck to create special conditions, instant replay. Terrific stat reporting includes analysis of starting cards, 3-D bar charts, graphs. Play interactively, run high speed simulation to test strategies. Hand Analyzer analyzes starting hands in detail. Wow!

**3. TURBO OMAHA HIGH-LOW SPLIT FOR WINDOWS - $89.95** -Specify any playing conditions; betting limits, number of raises, blind structures, button position, aggressiveness/passiveness of opponents, number of players (2-10), types of hands dealt, blinds, position, board reaction, specify flop, turn, river cards! Choose opponents, use provided point count or create your own. Statistical reporting, instant replay, pop-up odds, high speed simulation to test strategies, amazing Hand Analyzer, much more!

**4. TURBO OMAHA HIGH FOR WINDOWS - $89.95** - Same features as above, but tailored for the Omaha High-only game. Caro says program is "an electrifying research tool...it can clearly be worth thousands of dollars to any serious player. A must for Omaha High players.

**5. TURBO 7 STUD 8 OR BETTER - $89.95** - Brand new with all the features you expect from the Wilson Turbo products: the latest artificial intelligence, instant advice and exact odds, play versus 2-7 opponents, enhanced data charts that can be exported or printed, the ability to fold out of turn and immediately go to the next hand, ability to peek at opponents hand, optional warning mode that warns you if a play disagrees with the advisor, and automatic testing mode that can run up to 50 tests unattended. Challenge tough computer players who vary their styles for a truly great poker game.

---

**6. TOURNAMENT TEXAS HOLD'EM - $59.95**
Set-up for tournament practice and play, this realistic simulation pits you against celebrity look-alikes. Tons of options let you control tournament size with 10 to 300 entrants, select limits, ante, rake, blind structures, freezeouts, number of rebuys and competition level of opponents - average, tough, or toughest. Pop-up status report shows how you're doing vs. the competition. Save tournaments in progress to play again later. Additional feature allows you to quickly finish a folded hand and go on to the next.

# VIDEOS BY MIKE CARO
## THE MAD GENIUS OF POKER

### CARO'S PRO POKER TELLS

The long-awaited two-video set is a powerful scientific course on how to use your opponents' gestures, words and body language to read their hands and win all their money. These carefully guarded poker secrets, filmed with 63 poker notables, will revolutionize your game. It reveals when opponents are bluffing, when they aren't, and why. Knowing what your opponent's gestures mean, and protecting them from knowing yours, gives you a huge winning edge. An absolute must buy! $59.95.

### CARO'S MAJOR POKER SEMINAR

The legendary "Mad Genius" is at it again, giving poker advice in VHS format. This new tape is based on the inaugural class at Mike Caro University of Poker, Gaming and Life strategy. The material given on this tape is based on many fundamentals introduced in Caro's books, papers, and articles and is prepared in such a way that reinforces concepts old and new. Caro's style is easy-going but intense with key concepts stressed and repeated. This tape will improve your play. 60 Minutes. $24.95.

### CARO'S POWER POKER SEMINAR

This powerful video shows you how to win big money using the little-known concepts of world champion players. This advice will be worth thousands of dollars to you every year, even more if you're a big money player! After 15 years of refusing to allow his seminars to be filmed, Caro presents entertaining but serious coverage of his long-guarded secrets. Contains the most profitable poker advice ever put on video. 62 Minutes! $39.95.